OSWALD JACOBY AND JOHN R. CRAWFORD are very good friends and through the years have been amiable rivals in a variety of games.

At backgammon there are seven international championships: Jacoby has won three, Crawford one. Both still play.

Crawford has held five national bridge titles, and Jacoby was second to him in four of them. Crawford has also been a member of three of the five American teams to win the world's championship. Jacoby has won the world's championship once and is at present non-playing captain of the world's championship team. He also writes a syndicated bridge column and has won more national bridge championships than anyone else.

At other games, Jacoby will admit that Crawford is probably the best gin-rummy player in the world. But Jacoby is probably superior at casino and piquet. When it comes to bridge and backgammon, neither will concede to the other...

# The
# BACKGAMMON
# Book

## Oswald Jacoby

## John R. Crawford

**BANTAM BOOKS**
TORONTO · NEW YORK · LONDON · SYDNEY

*This low-priced Bantam Book
has been completely reset in a type face
designed for easy reading, and was printed
from new plates. It contains the complete
text of the original hard-cover edition.*
NOT ONE WORD HAS BEEN OMITTED.

THE BACKGAMMON BOOK

*A Bantam Book / published by arrangement with
The Viking Press, Inc.*

*PRINTING HISTORY*

*Viking edition published December 1970*

*Bantam edition / September 1973*

| | |
|---|---|
| 2nd printing . . . . . February 1974 | 8th printing . . . . September 1976 |
| 3rd printing . . . . . . . March 1974 | 9th printing . . . . . . March 1977 |
| 4th printing . . . . . September 1974 | 10th printing . . . . . . January 1978 |
| 5th printing . . . . . February 1975 | 11th printing . . . . . . August 1978 |
| 6th printing . . . . . . . . June 1975 | 12th printing . . . . . . . . May 1979 |
| 7th printing . . . . . . . October 1975 | 13th printing . . . . November 1979 |
| 14th printing . . . . . July 1980 | |

ACKNOWLEDGMENTS

*Many people helped, and it is a pleasure to thank them.*

*All the expert players whose names appear in this book, and many
others, helped us to develop the theories of play presented in herein.*

*The International Backgammon Association helped us with the laws and
the chapter on tournaments, as did G. W. E. (Joe) Baldwin and the other
members of the Interclub League of New York committee who worked with
us.*

*Owen Traynor and the Fort Lauderdale Backgammon Club gave us
pictures and material about their regular weekly tournaments.*

*Captain W. H. Benson, U.S.N. (Ret.)—who is also retired as Professor
of Mathematics at Dickinson College—helped check the entire man-
uscript, with particular attention to the parts dealing with probability.*

*Finally, this book would never have been finished without the tremen-
dous job done by Peter Kemeny and many others at The Viking Press. We
can't thank them enough.*

# CONTENTS

To the genius who invented the doubling cube
and made backgammon the game it is

# INTRODUCTION:
# THE HISTORY OF BACKGAMMON

The history of backgammon is long, complicated, very incomplete—and fascinating. The exact origins of the game remain unknown, though there is much conjecture, a good deal of it both ingenious and farfetched.

Backgammon is a dice game, and dice games seem to have developed in every part of the world. At first tribal priests rolled the bones of animals to predict the future. But since predicting the future is at best a hazardous business, it wasn't long before people began to roll the bones and bet on the outcome.

It is not hard to see how dice, our modern "bones," evolved. Our primitive ancestors may have carved four, eight, twelve, or twenty faces on their gambling bones, but there are two good reasons why the six-faced die—with numbers or pictures on each face—evolved fairly universally. The first is that it is rather easy to build a cube. The second is that the cubic form is best for rolling; a pyramid tends to stop fast when it hits, and an octahedron or a form with even more faces tends to roll too much.

Once dice had been invented, the next step was to use them to move game pieces around a game layout. Games of this kind seem to have developed everywhere, and some may be early ancestors of backgammon.

The most ancient possible ancestor of the game to be found so far dates back some five thousand years to the ancient civilization of Sumer which flourished in southern Mesopotamia in what is now Iraq. During the 1920s Sir Leonard Woolley, the British archaeologist, excavated Ur of the Chaldees, the Biblical home of Abraham. In the royal cemetery he found five game layouts which bear some slight resemblance to our backgammon boards. They

1

were made of wood, intricately decorated with a mosaic of shell, bone, lapis lazuli, red paste, and red limestone set in bitumen, and adorned with animals and rosettes.

Soon after Woolley's discovery, in another part of ancient Mesopotamia, archaeologists found a similar gaming board. This one was less lavishly decorated, but under the board, in neat piles, were found two sets of playing pieces and dice. One set of men consisted of simple black squares, each inlaid with five lapis dots; the others were shell squares engraved with animal vignettes. Each player apparently had seven men and six dice.

There is evidence that several thousand years later the Egyptian Pharaohs were enjoying another board game that may be an ancestor of backgammon. Boards dating from 1500 B.C. were found in King Tutankhamen's tomb in the valley of the Nile, and even at Enkomi on Cyprus, then an Egyptian colony. One board contains Queen Hatshepsut's name, and with the board were found lion-headed pieces, the ancient symbols of royal power. Wall paintings in many Egyptian tombs portray people playing the game, suggesting that it was played by common people as well as by the aristocracy.

However much the Egyptian game differs from what has evolved into modern backgammon, the Egyptians had one bit of equipment we might envy: a mechanical dice box. The dice were put into it, shaken up, and thrown out onto the table. Like everyone else, the ancient Egyptians played their game for money and invented this machine to guard against cheaters (always a sign of higher civilization). The Greeks and Romans later adopted this device in their versions of the game.

But where did the first versions of backgammon originate? We don't know and may never know; a reasonable guess would be India or China, the two civilizations we have inherited most games from.

Each produced a game of pure skill. The Indian game was chess. The Chinese played a version similar enough to show that there must have been commerce across the Himalayas. But the connection between either version of chess and backgammon is tenuous indeed.

There is, however, sufficient similarity between backgammon and another ancient Indian game, parcheesi, to suggest the latter as a possible remote ancestor. Parcheesi is primarily a four-person game, played on a board, in which each player has several identical men. Unlike modern backgammon, the men start *off* the board (as they do in the Navy game of acey-deucy and in some other forms of backgammon). In parcheesi a player who rolls a doublet makes his play and then takes an extra roll; in acey-deucy a player who rolls an ace-deuce (1–2) plays it and any double he wishes, and then gets an extra roll; in backgammon a doublet number is played four times, which is the same as two plays.

The object in parcheesi, as in backgammon, is to "bear off" all your men from the board, and in both games a player must bring all of his men into his home sector before he can start to bear them off. Further, in both games a single man or "blot" is a weakness since an opponent can play to that point and send that man off the board. And in both games two or more men on a point are very strong; in parcheesi even more so than in backgammon, since an opponent may not even pass such a point.

A number of versions of backgammon can be found throughout the Far East. In China there is the game called *shwan-liu*. In Japan they play *sunoroku*, which omits the bar. In Korea they play *ssang-ryouk;* in Thailand, *len sake* or *saka;* and in Malaya, *main tabal*.

But the game must have reached Western Europe from the Mediterranean. A thousand years after the Egyptians were playing their version, the Greeks, or at least the patrician Greeks, were playing a form of the game. Plato mentions a Greek form of the game and comments on its popularity. Sophocles attributes its invention to Palamedes, who was said to have beguiled away the time during the long siege of Troy by playing it. Homer mentions the Greek game in the *Odyssey*. Herodotus claims that the Lydians invented it.

In this and other dice games the Greeks evidently had feelings about lady luck just as strong as ours. They called sixes, which were good high rolls then as now, "Aphrodite," and they called ones a word akin to "dog."

In Rome the game long remained one of the most popular among the patricians. It rivaled the Circus Maximus as a pastime and was regarded as the sport of emperors. Indeed, the excavators of Pompeii found a backgammon table carved in the courtyard of almost every villa.

The game had three names in Rome and was apparently played with three dice instead of our two. It was called *"alea,"* or dice; *"tabulae,"* or tables; and the more descriptive name of *"ludus duodecim scriptorum,"* the twelve-line game, for the twelve points on each side of the board.

Though Julius Caesar may have said *"Alea jacta est"* (the die is cast) when he crossed the Rubicon, there is no evidence that he played any particular dice game. Other Roman emperors did, however; one even had a special room in his palace designed for dicing. And according to Suetonius, the emperor Claudius was so fond of the game that he wrote a book on it—and had a table mounted on his chariot so he could play while traveling! There are also records that say Domitian was an expert player—and that Caligula was a cheat. And there are reports, fanciful or otherwise, that Marc Antony played *ludus duodecim scriptorum* with Cleopatra.

Apparently some resourceful Romans also used the game to play a classical version of strip poker. A painted glass exists that depicts a young man and a girl seated in front of a backgammon board; they are partially undressed, and nearby on the floor are pieces of clothing. The inscription, *"Devincavi,"* means "I think I've beaten you."

Nero, among his other excesses, is said to have played the game for as much as the equivalent of 15,000 dollars a point. The emperor Commodus is reported to have turned the imperial palace into a grandiose gambling casino. Indeed, it is recorded that at one point he was losing so badly that he appropriated a large sum from the imperial treasury, ostensibly to finance an expedition to the African provinces, promptly went back to the tables, and lost every cent.

At Pompeii a fascinating wall painting was found portraying a backgammon tale in two scenes. In the first, two players are arguing over a game in progress; the second depicts an innkeeper throwing the two fighting opponents out of his establishment. So the game was apparently enjoyed by ordinary Romans as well as the aristocracy.

4

The game continued to be played in Rome after the establishment of Christianity. A marble slab was found among the Christian artifacts in Rome in which a backgammon board had been carved; in the center is a Greek cross, and there is an inscription which roughly means "Our Lord Jesus Christ grants aid and victory to dicers if they write his Name when they roll the dice, Amen."

The Roman legions must have brought *tabulae* with them through Europe. But except for the fact that the name survived in Britain as "tables," it does not appear that Rome's conquered lands were immediately receptive. It seems to have been the return of the Crusaders that effectively spread the game throughout Europe.

At least one form of backgammon was played in the Middle East long before the Crusades. The source may have been ancient Sumer, Egypt, India, or all three, but the game the Crusaders encountered among the Saracens—and enthusiastically adopted—was called *nard* or *nard-shir*. The Arabs had learned the game from the Persians, and it was supposedly named after Ard-shir Babakan of the Sassanid dynasty of the ancient Persian empire, who was said to have invented it. Using two dice instead of the Roman three, the game was played on a checkered cloth that contained twelve divisions corresponding to the solar months of the Persian year. The total number of men, or *muhrahs*, corresponded to the number of days in the lunar month; half the counters were black and half were white, since during half the month the nights were dark and during the other half the nights were brightly lit by the moon. The names of the seven points in the game were richly suggestive: *Kad* (quantity), *Ziyad* (growth), *Satarah* (fortune, curtain or veil, or star), *Hazaran* (thousands), *Khanah-gir* (possessor of the house or chamber), *Tawil* (tall, or long), and *Mansubah* (scheme, plan, or game).

Various early versions of backgammon seem to have been popular in Britain. Though the game was known in Anglo-Saxon times and is mentioned in old English glossaries of the eighth and ninth centuries, its great popularity apparently dates from the Crusades.

In fact, this and other gambling games were so popular with the Christian soldiers in Richard the Lion-Hearted's army that he and his ally, Philip of France, issued a joint edict during the Third Crusade in 1190. In the words of the historian Joseph Strutt, whose book *Sports and Pastimes of the People of England* was published in 1841: "It prohibits any person in the army beneath the degree of a knight from playing at any sort of game for money: knights and clergymen might play for money, but no one of them was permitted to lose more than twenty shillings in one whole day and night, under the penalty of one hundred shillings, to be paid to the archbishops in the army; the two monarchs had the privilege of playing for what they pleased; but their attendants were restricted to the sum of twenty shillings; and if they exceeded, they were to be whipped naked through the army for three days."

Richard's brother, King John, also liked to play the game, which by now had acquired its English name "tables," after the Roman *tabulae*. King John played his court favorites for modest stakes; if he lost, the amount was faithfully noted in the record of his daily expenses.

It remained a favorite game of the upper classes in Europe throughout the middle ages. Robert of Gloucester's thirteenth-century chronicle portrays knights playing "atte tables," and there is a similar passage in the *Song of Roland*.

Tables spread from the upper classes throughout medieval society in Europe. Innkeepers attracted customers by providing them with boards, men, and dice. Apparently the medieval board was twice the size of the usual chessboard, and the men were larger than our modern playing discs.

The Church, which of course did not approve of any kind of gambling, waged a long and losing war against the popular game. In 1254 Louis IX of France (Saint Louis) forbade the game to his court officials and extended the ban to all his subjects. One hundred and fifty years later the Archbishop of Tournai was busy prosecuting people caught playing tables. The schools of Bologna decided that ecclesiastical canons did not apply to chess—but tables was still classified with the *"inhonesti ludi"* (dishonest, or dishonorable, games), and attempts to suppress it continued until the end of the fifteenth century.

6

By then, towns in France, Italy, Spain, Switzerland, and Holland were exempting tables from municipal censure so long as the stakes were kept small. However, the game remained forbidden to university students and apprentices learning their trade.

One scholarly sleuth, H. J. R. Murray, has discovered at least twenty-five different kinds of "tables" played in various parts of Europe during the Middle Ages. In an article on "The Medieval Game of Backgammon," he wrote:

> In Spain and England the game *emperador,* or the *English game,* stands out as the leading variety of tables, in Germany *buf,* in the Low Countries and Scandinavian countries *verkeer* or *kotra.* . . . *Testa* was the game most frequently played in Italy. . . . In France *tric-trac,* which has a certain resemblance to the Spanish *laquet,* came to the front from about 1500.
>
> The most interesting of these games is *emperador,* because both in Spain and England there were special terms for different ways of winning, comparable to the distinctions made in modern backgammon between the win, the gammon, and the backgammon. In Spain, the blocking of six consecutive points gave the winner *barata;* in England there were two special wins known as *limpolding* and *lurching.*

We suspect that, in mentioning "lurching," Mr. Murray may have confused backgammon and cribbage boards. Though cribbage is a card game, the score is kept by moving pegs around the board as points are made. The first man to score 121 wins, and if his opponent's more advanced peg has not yet reached the home board (the last 30 holes), the loser has been "left in the lurch," or "lurched," and loses double the stake.

The modern board appears in pictures in Europe as early as the fourteenth century, and after that widely throughout the continent as the game flourished and spread. Very ornate boards survive from this period, and even church decorations—some of Germany's medieval cathedrals contain depictions of backgammon boards. And there were many treatises and illuminated manuscripts to explain the game.

English history and literature are full of references to tables and, later, backgammon. One fourteenth-century English tract describes, in Latin, several different *"ludi ad tabulas."* Here is one interesting variation, translated by Strutt:

> There are many methods of playing at the tables with the dice. The first of these, and the longest, is called the English game, *Ludus Anglicorum,* which is thus performed: he who sits on the side of the board marked 1–12 has fifteen men in the part [point] marked 24, and he who sits on the side marked 13–24 has a like number of men in the part 1. They play with three dice or else with two (allowing always [a roll of] six for a third dice). Then he who is seated at 1–12 must bring all his men placed at 24 through the partitions from 24 to 19, from 18 to 13, and from 12 to 7, into the division 6–1, and then bear them off; his opponent must do the same from 1 to 7, thence to 12, thence to 18, into the compartment 19–24; and he who bears off all his men is conquerer.

The same treatise goes on to describe other variations of tables, including *Paume Carie,* played with two dice and four players.

Chaucer alludes to the game in *The Canterbury Tales:* "They daucen, and they pleyen at ches and tables." Spenser refers to it in *The Faerie Queene,* and in *Love's Labours Lost* Shakespeare has Biron say:

> "This is the ape of the form,
> Monsieur the Nice,
> that, when he plays at table,
> chides the dice
> in honourable terms."

In 1579 John Northbrooke published a sober treatise reproving "idle pastimes" on the Sabbath Day "by the authoritie of the worde of God and ancient writers." He has rather a good word to say for our game, or at least he condemns it with faint praise: "Playing at tables is far more tollerable (although in all respects not allowable) than Dice and Cards are, for that it leaneth partlie to chance, and partlie to industrie of the mind."

At least Northbrooke recognized that tables was a game of skill, and perhaps his attitude was more liberal than it looks, since as recently as 1526 Cardinal Wolsey had decreed that all tables, dice, cards, and bowls were illegal and should be burnt.

However, since people are both stubborn and resourceful, some artisans disguised backgammon boards as books—inside were dice, men, and dice boxes.

The game continued to flourish at royal courts, even in Scotland. James the First is reputed to have spent the last evening of his life, before his murder in 1437, "in reading with his Queen and the nobles and ladies of his Court, and in playing at Chess and Tables."

The tables were turned, so to speak, in 1479, when the Duke of Albany, brother of James III of Scotland, was confined in Edinburgh Castle. One night he invited the captain of the guard to supper, and they spent a jovial evening drinking, singing, and playing at tables. In the morning the royal captive had disappeared, and his jailer was dead.

The game remained one of the most popular sports among the Elizabethans. A generation later King James I of England observed, in *A Kinge's Christian Dutie Towards God*, the interminably moralistic guide book he wrote for his eldest son, Henry, the future king: "As for sitting, or house pastimes—since they may at times supply the roome, which, being emptie, would be patent to pernicious idleness—I will not therefore agree with the curiositie of some learned men of our age in forbidding cardes, dice, and such like games of hazard; when it is foule and stormie weather, then I say, may ye lawfully play at cardes or tables."

And apparently the game continued to flourish among lesser folk, in fair as well as "foule and stormie" weather. Robert Burton, in *The Anatomy of Melancholy*, gives a

9

general view of seventeenth-century sports: "Ordinary recreations we have in winter, as cards, tables, dice, shovel-board, chess-lay . . ."

The earliest recorded use of the word "backgammon" was in 1645, according to the *Oxford Universal Dictionary*. H. J. R. Murray, in *A History of Board Games Other Than Chess*, says that backgammon, the modern form of tables, was invented in England early in the seventeenth century. The two differences between backgammon and tables that Murray lists are slight but very interesting: in backgammon (1) doublets are now played twice, and (2) the triple game, or backgammon, is introduced and defined thus: "when the winner bears all his men before his opponent has carried all his men to his home or bearing table." This is more like our gammon than our triple game, but it's getting there!

Tables was still the more common name used throughout the seventeenth century. As late as September 21, 1665, Samuel Pepys wrote in his diary: "I got to my Lord Bruncker's before night, and there I sat and supped with him and his mistresse. . . . Thence, after losing a crowne betting at Tables, we walked home."

Thirteen years later Samuel Butler mentioned backgammon in his satirical epic poem *Hudibras,* which may be the first use of the word in English literature.

There are a number of possible sources for the word "backgammon." For example, in Welsh *bach* means small, and *cammaun* means battle. But since in many early versions of the game players began with all the men off the board, a less interesting but more plausible source is Middle English: *baec* means back, *gamen* means game— i.e., a game in which (1) you want to go back home and back off the board again, and (2) you may be forced back (to the bar) and to start over. Or perhaps it simply came from the fact that most chessboards were marked for backgammon on the back.

A historian writing over a century ago noted that "at the commencement of the eighteenth century backgammon was a very favorite amusement, and pursued at leisure times by most persons of opulence, and especially by the clergy." In fact, the game was so popular among his fellow clergymen that Dean Swift once advised a friend in the country, with tongue in cheek, to study the game "that he might be on friendly, that is playing, terms with the rector. . . . And certainly debates about hits were easier of settlement than disputes about tithes from Sir Roger de Coverley—who when he wished to obtain from the University a chaplain of piety and urbanity, in short a Christian minister, conditioned that he should know something about backgammon." Sir Roger was of course Addison and Steele's fictitious country gentleman, whose exploits entertained the readers of *The Spectator*.

And in 1735 Soame Jenyns composed the following verse:

> Here you'll be ever sure to meet
> A hearty welcome, though no treat;
> A house where quiet guards the door,
> Nor rural wits smoke, drink, and roar;
> Choice books, safe horses, wholesome liquor
> Billiards, backgammon, and the vicar.

Another writer with a practical bent proclaimed backgammon "an anodyne to the gout, the rheumatism, the azure devils or the yellow spleen." A more snobbish and equally inaccurate fan contended that "from time immemorial, backgammon has held the foremost position among the elite of popular games. It has ever been a game for the higher classes and has never been vulgarized or defiled by uneducated people."

And Hoyle, of course, wrote a treatise on the game which first appeared in 1743, the year after his book on whist.

During the nineteenth century interest in the game seems to have waned somewhat, though there are still literary references early in the century. Sir Walter Scott, one of the fashion-setters of his time, was an enthusiastic player, and Lord Byron wrote in *Don Juan:* "Like a backgammon board, the place was dotted with whites and blacks."

In the middle of the nineteenth century a historian of games named George Frederick Pardon wrote a book on backgammon (following in the grand tradition of Hoyle, his book appeared the year after he wrote one on whist).

In it he made a valiant, relentless, and typically Victorian attempt to sell the game to the middle classes. Here is a particularly inspiring excerpt, in his inimitable prose:

> The technical terms of backgammon may teach valuable lessons. . . . In the game, it is proper to "get your men to your table," and to effect it as rapidly as possible; *that* teaches hospitality, brisk as its own champagne.
>
> "Cover your man" is another maxim; *that* shows protection must be afforded to the helpless, clothing to him "whose looped and *windowed* raggedness" demands payment of such charitable imposts; 'tis, moreover, to diminish the amount of poor's-rate, by encouraging manufactures, and let political economists prescribe a better remedy!
>
> "Get home as quickly as you can" inculcates the culture of domestic happiness; and suggests a speedy return from even the most festive scenes, in order to light up eyes that such return renders brighter than the tapers by which the loved one waits and muses.
>
> "Go back" is often said at backgammon, and should be the endeavor of the wanderer from the path of rectitude, ere the *second* false step has been taken.

Despite Mr. Pardon (who wisely published his book under the pseudonym Captain Rawdon Crawley), the game remained a favorite of the English upper classes, and it was played constantly in the nineteenth century in their many clubs and country houses.

Though probably less popular than in Britain, backgammon has been played in the United States since the seventeenth century. Thomas Jefferson played the game often—including during the three weeks before July 4, 1776, while he was drafting the Declaration of Independence. He kept a notebook of his expenses, and among the entries are these two:

> Lost at backgammon 7/6.
> Won at backgammon 7d/1/3.

Records survive from the mid-nineteenth century revealing that at least one of the Mississippi riverboat gamblers used a portable backgammon set to fleece victims on board the famed *Natchez.*

In France the game has continued to be called "trictrac," a phonetic name for the sound made as the men were moved around the originally wooden board. An eighteenth-century French writer observed that "tric-trac was a game played by old men and scholars, although at the court of Paris it was played often and considered a game of nobility and distinction." The typical gentleman of Louis XIII's reign was described as playing tric-trac on a chest covered with an oriental rug, on which the board rested. And in 1682 *Le Mercure* described the Sun King's new apartments at Versailles, in which were discovered: "A pentagonal table, a square one, a triangular one—all were used by the King and Queen to play on. All were covered with green velvet and gold embroidery and dressed with silver candlesticks."

A century later, during the era of Louis XVI and Marie Antoinette, specially designed tric-trac tables began to appear in the homes of the French aristocracy. The trictrac table looked like a small, flat desk; the center was hollow and contained the game itself. On the sides, little holes were made to hold ivory or silver flags that indicated the points. There were drawers for the pieces, the dice, and dice cups, and the top was covered with felt for playing cards on one side, and the other had a chessboard or a leather surface to be used as a desk. These tables were fantastically intricate, inlaid with precious materials, and one table said to have been owned by Marie Antoinette cost 238,000 francs in gold.

The Italians called the game *"tavole reale,"* and the Spanish *"tablas reales";* both mean "royal tables." The Spanish are said to have learned the game from their Moorish conquerors.

In Germany the French name "tric-trac" was generally adopted. A book on ancient games published in 1892 gives the following rather dizzying account of something called "German Backgammon":

The Entering division and the *Home* are common to both players. The Entering division must be either the right-hand near division, or the left-hand opposite division.

The pieces enter by throws, and all pieces must be entered before any leave the Entering division.

On throwing doublets the player, after playing those doublets, is entitled to play the doublets underneath, which are always the complement of seven. Should he forget to do so, or should he not be able to do so, his opponent says—"I play your aces," or whatever the number may be.

On throwing 1, 2, the player can call for any doublets he chooses: but should he forget to do so, his opponent may say—"I play your doublets." But this must be done after throwing his dice, but not lifting up the dice-box.

This is an amusing game, not merely from the frequency of taking up, owing to the pieces all travelling in the same direction, but also from a player being permitted to play whatever his opponent cannot play; and also whatever his opponent forgets to play. The game is much longer than the ordinary backgammon, and the fluctuations of the game much greater, thus producing greater excitement.

Versions of the game are played in every European country. A so-called "Russian Backgammon" described in the *Encyclopædia Britannica* sounds strikingly like so-called "German Backgammon":

All stones are off the board at the outset, and are entered in the same table and travel concurrently around to the same home table. Variants differ as to other rules. The first stone entered may be moved thereafter, or two men must be entered before moving. Blots may be hit at any time; usually a blot must be re-entered before any other play is legal. Doublets are used twice over, together with the doublets on the opposite faces (opposite faces of a die total seven); sometimes the opposite doublets may be used first, and sometimes the caster may roll a second time after throwing doublets. This privilege is lost if he cannot use all of his first roll, and sometimes his opponent is allowed to use what he cannot. Complementary doublets and the second roll are usually barred on the first turn.

When the Spanish arrived in Mexico early in the sixteenth century, they were astounded to find the Aztecs playing a game called *patolli*, which has enough points in common with some ancient precursors of backgammon and similar board games in Asia that anthropologists sometimes cite the fact as evidence to support the theory that the Indian tribes of the Western Hemisphere originally migrated from Asia.

In *The Daily Life of the Aztecs*, published in 1961, the distinguished scholar Jacques Soustelle described the ancient Aztec game:

> *Patolli* was a game with dice, not unlike our game of *ludi* [Roman backgammon]. The *Codex Magliabecchiano* shows four players sitting on the ground or on mats round a table shaped like a cross and divided into squares. At one side there is the god Macuilxochitl, tutelary diety of dancing, music, and gambling, watching over them.
>
> For dice the players use beans called patolli, marked with a certain number of pips; and according to the numbers thrown, they move small colored stones from square to square on the board. The winner of the game and the stakes was the one who first came back to the square he had started from.
>
> Patolli . . . had a hidden inner meaning. There were fifty-two squares on the board, that is, the same number as the years that are contained by the combined divinatory and solar cycles. . . .
>
> Patolli . . . was the most generally played game in all classes, and in it the Indians' passion for gambling could run unchecked. It is still played—or at least it was still played twenty years ago, among the Nahua and Totonac Indians of the Sierra de Puebla.

Backgammon is still widely played in the eastern Mediterranean countries, by all classes and kinds of people, from Rumanian fishermen to Greek aristocrats. In 1930 Georges Mabardi, an Egyptian who ran a popular *boîte* for thirsty New Yorkers, wrote a book on backgammon. Here is his description of the perfect backgammon player:

"The perfect backgammoner? Why, every day on the *terrasse* of the Café Bellevue, overlooking the blue Mediterranean—in Alexandria, my home—I have seen hundreds of perfect backgammoners, playing all day long. From the cradle to the grave, Egyptians play backgammon, the game of the Great Pharaohs. They play well, they play rapidly, they play quietly; they smile and talk a little and they never complain of their luck. They smoke their *narguilés* and drink their *café turc*. They believe that 'luck' is the just, the inevitable, reward of the skillful."

It would be strange indeed if our game of backgammon were the only game played on the backgammon board. There are many variations, including Russian backgammon and Persian backgammon, but they are especially numerous in the Mediterranean countries. There are the Turkish games of *moultezim* and *gioul*, the Greek *plakoto* and *eureika*, and countless others, including the U.S. navy game of acey-deucy, which originated in the Middle East.

In the United States and Europe interest in backgammon greatly revived in the 1920s when some unknown genius playing in one of the American clubs came up with a revolutionary idea. He proposed that, at his turn to play, a player might insist on doubling the stakes. His opponent would have the right to refuse, in which case the game would then end and be scored at the original stake.

Until this simple but ingenious innovation, there were just too many games in which the outcome would pretty much be decided in the first couple of rolls—yet play would have to go on interminably since there is always a chance of the unusual happening when the unpredictable dice are rolled. With doubles, the game could still be boring, of course, but it would be boring at doubled stakes. More important, lots of doubles would be refused and new games started more quickly. Thus, doubling increases the risk of winning and losing, and also adds the suspense and excitement of the dare, and sometimes the bluff, to the game.

This same inventive genius, or perhaps a second one, added the *redoubling* feature, which allows a player who has been doubled to redouble his opponent in the same manner, whenever it is his turn to roll the dice.

Doubling and redoubling has really livened up the game—and we have no hesitation in saying that backgammon is now undoubtedly *the most exciting gambling game there is!*

After the introduction of doubling, the game rapidly began to increase in popularity among clubmen, but there was one great problem: there were no laws for the game that were of any value. Each group settled disputed points in accord with their own best judgment, but there were no commonly accepted rules.

Among places where the game became exteremely popular was New York's Racquet and Tennis Club. In 1931 Wheaton Vaughan, chairman of the club's Card and Backgammon Committee, decided to undertake the task of preparing laws for the game. First he wrote to all other clubs that might be interested to ask them to send representatives to meetings. Those in the New York metropolitan area did so, and many others announced their willingness to abide by whatever laws were formulated.

The committee met, worked, and prepared laws, which have remained the accepted rules until now. As far as we know, Oswald Jacoby is the only member of that committee still living.

Those laws were good, but not perfect. Some are honored far more in the breach than in the observance. We have taken the liberty of preparing new laws in conjunction with the International Backgammon Association and the Interclub League of New York that we hope will replace these earlier laws.

Backgammon received another boost when Prince Alexis Obolensky conceived the idea of an international backgammon tournament. This tournament has been held in the Bahamas every year since 1964. The first attracted forty entries and was won by Charles Wacker of Chicago. The next was won by John Crawford, and the following three by Oswald Jacoby, and the last two by Walter Cooke. Each year has seen more entries in the championship, and more entries in the beginners' tournament.

The idea of holding backgammon tournaments is spreading rapidly. Obolensky conducted similar events at Las Vegas, and there have been other tournaments in London and Estoril, Portugal. We'll have more to say on tournaments, their players, and winners in Chapter 15.

More and more people all over the world are taking up this wonderful game, and we hope that this book will help many more to discover the fun and excitement of playing backgammon.

April 1970                                                    O. J. and J. C.

# 1

# FOR BEGINNERS

Whether or not you have ever watched a backgammon game, you almost certainly have seen a backgammon board. Most checkerboards are marked on the back with the twenty-four triangular "points" of a backgammon board.

The basic necessities for backgammon are:

*Two players.*

*A backgammon board.* Boards are obtainable in a wide range of materials, from a simple one costing a few dollars to expensive ones made of inlaid ivory and wood. There are also extremely valuable antique boards and tables.

*Thirty men or checkers,* half of them in one color and half in another. For convenience we will use the most common colors, white and black, throughout the book.

*A pair of dice.* The game is more fun if you have four dice instead of two (so each player may have a pair), and a couple of dice cups.

*A doubling cube.* This is needed only in a gambling game or tournament. It is an oversized die with the numbers 2, 4, 8, 16, 32, and 64 on the six faces, to help keep score. More on this in Chapter 7.

## The Setup of the Game

In learning the game it is best to set up the board immediately. We urge you to do so now and to work out each step of our discussion on your board as we go along. Diagram 1 shows a board set up for the start of play. Note that the board is divided into four quadrants, an inner (or home) table and an outer table for each player. The

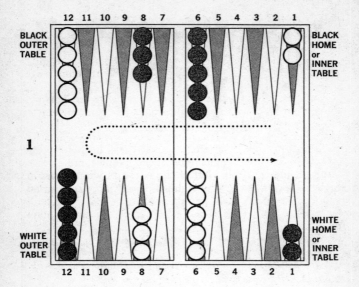

BLACK OUTER TABLE

BLACK HOME or INNER TABLE

WHITE OUTER TABLE

WHITE HOME or INNER TABLE

1

12  11  10  9  8  7    6  5  4  3  2  1

upper right hand quadrant has been set up as black's inner table, the upper left as black's outer table, the lower right as white's inner table, and the lower left as white's outer table. Inner and outer tables are also called inner and outer boards.

Each table is divided into six triangular "points" colored alternately in two contrasting colors, usually red and gray, to facilitate counting. Backgammon boards come in all sizes and colors. So do the men. All that is necessary is that the colors of alternate points and of opposing men be contrasting.

In our diagram the points in the inner boards are numbered from one to six, and in the outer boards from seven to twelve. There is a total of twenty-four points, and you play the game by moving your men from point to point according to numbers rolled on the dice. The points are not numbered on your actual board, nor are the inner and

20

outer boards labeled as such. To help you learn the game we urge you to memorize this information as quickly as possible.

The middle strip that divides the board into the inner and outer tables is called the "bar"; the number seven points are called the "bar points."

Technically it does not matter in which direction you move your men, and the board could be set up in exactly the opposite way, as a mirror image of the first: white's inner board becomes his outer board, his one point becomes his twelve point, etc., and play goes in the opposite direction. The bar points (the seven points) are now to the right instead of the left of the bar, and white bears off to the left instead of the right. There is no strategic advantage whatever to either setup; the more common setup evolved out of ancient custom that the inner board should be nearer the source of light. Today, with modern lighting, the alternate setup may be used if both players agree before setting up the game. Throughout this book we will use the more common setup illustrated in Diagram 1.

## The Object of the Game

Throughout this book you will be white, and your objective will be to move your men around the board in the direction shown by the arrow in Diagram 1 (you cannot move backward) until you bring them all into your inner board and bear them off. Only when all fifteen of your men are in your inner board can you start taking them off the board, which is called "bearing off." Your opponent moves his men in the opposite direction and eventually bears them off from his inner board. The man who first bears off all his men wins the game.

## Preliminaries to Play

Most of the time two players merely sit down, set up the men, and begin to play. If there is any question as to choice of colors, seats, or directions in which to move around the board, you roll for high dice to settle it.

At the start of any later game, you may roll for the same choices, although this is seldom done.

## Starting to Play

The laws of backgammon provide that each man throws a single die to decide who plays first. The one rolling the higher number makes the first play by moving the numbers shown on the two dice—his own and his opponent's. If both players throw the same number, they continue to throw until they get different ones.

By mutual agreement in many friendly games, the high roller is allowed the option of throwing again if he does not care for the first roll. We do not recommend this or other variations, but they will be discussed thoroughly in Chapter 16.

After the first move players alternate turns.

## Cocked Dice

Each player throws his two dice onto the board at his right. Unless both dice come to rest flat on the board and not on any of the men, the dice are deemed to be cocked and there must be a rethrow.

## What Constitutes a Play

A player moves his men according to the numbers shown on the dice he has thrown. The numbers are considered *individually,* not in sum total. Thus, he may move the whole throw with one man or each of the two numbers with different men; either number may be played first. For example, a throw that shows 5 on one die and 3 on the other is considered a 5-and-3 move, or a 3-and-5 move, but not an 8 move. One man may be moved five points and another three points, or a single man may first be moved five and then three points (or first three and then five points).

If he rolls a double (i.e., both dice showing the same number) he moves that number four times. If he rolls double 2, for example, he may move two points four times, in any possible combination:

Any one man may be moved a total of eight points.

Any two men may be moved a total of four points each.

Any two men may be moved two points each, and another man a total of four points.

Any one man may be moved a total of six points, and another man two points.

Any four men may be moved two points each.

Keep in mind that whenever you make more than one play with a single man you are actually playing two (or more in case of a doublet) *separate* moves and not one total move. The same rules apply to any intermediate stop, called "touching down," as apply to your final landing, or occupying, spot.

## Points

You may occupy or touch down on any triangle that is unoccupied, or one already occupied by one or more of your own men. If a triangle has only one of your opponent's men on it (called a "blot"—see below) he is vulnerable and you may touch down or land there, sending him off the board. This is called a "hit," and your opponent's man must re-enter and begin moving around the board again.

If a triangle has two or more of your opponent's men on it, he has "made that point," and those men are safe from attack. They cannot be hit, and you may not occupy or touch down on that triangle. In the same way, when you can move two or more of your men to the same unoccupied triangle (or a triangle with only one of your opponent's men on it) you are said to be "making a point."

In the opening setup (Diagram 1) you—white—hold your own six and eight points and your opponent's twelve and one points. If you threw 3–1, you would probably move one man three triangles from your eight point to your five point and another man one triangle from your six point to your five point, thereby "making your five point." You are allowed to move any number of extra men to a point that you have already made, but you may *never* move one of your men to a point that your opponent holds with two or more of his men.

23

# Primes

Since each play is composed of two individual moves (or four individual moves when you roll doubles), each triangle or point that you have "made" increases your ability to impede your adversary's play. Six "made" points in a row constitute what is known as a "prime" and completely block any move past them, since any of the numbers from 1 to 6 that could be thrown would land on one of your controlled points.

# The Moves

There are three types of moves: moving men around the board; entering men from the bar; and bearing men off the board.

As we have said, when moving a single man more than once in a roll, technically you are touching down on the spaces indicated on the dice. Thus, you may not touch down on a point controlled by your opponent, even though the number on your other die would carry you beyond it. For example, if your opponent controls both his six and seven (bar) points and you throw 6–5, you cannot move a man from his one point to his twelve point, since it is impossible for you to move either 6 or 5. If, on the other hand, he controls his seven point but his six point is open, you could first move 5, touching down on his open six point, and then 6 to his twelve point.

A player must make his full move, playing all the numbers thrown, if it is possible for his men to do so anywhere on the board. This can be hazardous, since you may be forced to leave one or more men exposed as a blot, or to weaken your position in some other way. If you can move either of the two numbers (but in neither case can you move the second number), you must move the larger one. If you can move both numbers, you may move either number first.

# Blots

As we have noted, when you have only one man on a point, that man is known as a blot, and your opponent is free to play to that point. If he does so, he is said to be "hitting your blot."

## The Bar

After hitting your blot, your opponent picks up the man he has hit and places it on the bar in the center of the board. That man is said to have been "sent off the board," or "back home," or "to the bar," and he remains on the bar until he can be entered in your opponent's inner table by a throw of the dice. Similarly, your opponent must re-enter on your inner table any blots that you may hit. It is possible for both players to have men on the bar at the same time, or for one player to have several men on the bar. If a player has one or more men on the bar, he must enter *all* of them before moving any other men. This may cause him to miss his whole throw.

## Entering from the Bar

You can enter men from the bar if the number on *one* of your two dice corresponds to any point in your opponent's inner board that he does not control with two or more men.

If, for example, you throw 4–3 and your opponent does not control either his four or his three points, you can enter on either of these points. If he controls the four point, you must enter on the three point, and vice versa.

If your opponent controls all six points in his inner board, you cannot enter a man from the bar. Since you may not move any other man while you have a man on the bar, you miss your turn and need not bother to throw the dice at all.

Even when your opponent holds only one point in his inner board you may miss your whole play. Suppose it is early in the game; your opponent has hit one of your blots and sent it to the bar, and he controls only the six point in his inner board. If you roll double 6s, you cannot enter and you miss your play.

Remember, you *can* enter on a point in your opponent's home board that is: (1) vacant; (2) already occupied by one or more of your own men; or (3) occupied by one of your opponent's men. You can hit this blot like any other, sending him off the board to the bar. He must then re-enter on *your* home board.

You *cannot* come in on any point held by two or more of your opponent's men.

## Bearing Off

You begin the game with five of your fifteen men already in your inner table, and your first goal is to get the rest of them in there. Once you've done so, you can begin bearing them off the board. If you are the first to bear off all your men, you win the game.

After all your men are in your inner table, you bear them off according to the dice you throw. If you throw 5–3, for example, you can remove one man from the five point and one from the three point. If your throw is a double, you are as usual entitled to twice the value; thus, if you roll double 3, you can remove four men from your three point.

You must use your entire roll if possible, *or as much of it as you can*. That is, if you throw a 6 on one die but have no men on your six point, you must take a man off the highest point on which you do have men: if you have a man on the five point, you must remove him; if you have none on the six or five point but have a man on the four point, you must remove him, and so on.

The same rule applies with doubles. Let's say you have two men on the six point, none on the five point, and one man each on the four and three points. If you roll double 6, you can take all four of these men off: removing the two sixes leaves the four your highest point still occupied, so you can use one of your two remaining moves to take him off; this in turn leaves the man on your three point the highest remaining, so you can bear him off with your last 6.

As we will see more fully in Chapter 5, there are times when you may prefer to move inside your inner table in-stead of bearing off—particularly when your opponent has one or more men in your inner table, trying for an eleventh-hour hit. You can move inside your inner table instead of bearing off if—and only if—by doing so you can still use all of the number you have thrown. For example, say you have a man on each of your six, five, three, and two points, and your opponent has two men on your four point. You roll 3–2. You could bear off the men on your three and two points, but you'd be wiser to move the men on your six and five points down past your opponent's men to your three point. In another situation you may want to move one man within your inner board and bear off another, which you can do as long as by doing so you are still using all the numbers that you have rolled.

If your opponent hits you while you're bearing off, you must as usual re-enter from the bar, and get that man back to your inner board before you can resume bearing off more men.

## Winning

There are three degrees of winning:

A normal victory, where the loser has been able to bear off at least one of his men. The winner scores the amount at stake.

A "gammon," where the loser has not been able to bear off any of his men. The winner scores double the stake.

A "backgammon," when the loser hasn't taken off any men and has one or more of his men stuck in the winner's inner table or on the bar. The winner scores three times the stake.

## The Early Game

Each point you make constitutes a block against any opposing men who may want to pass it. So one of your principal aims must be to make points to block your opponent's progress—give him as few places as possible on which to land. Another principal aim must be to get your back men (the two men on black one point in Diagram 1) off and running.

These two objectives constitute your rules of play for the early game: get your back men out, and block your opponent's back men. The various strategies you may want to employ in moving your men around the board as the game develops will be discussed in logical sequence in subsequent chapters. For now, we have simply wanted to make the mechanics of the game clear to you. When you have thoroughly mastered them, you'll be ready to go on to our discussion of the opening move.

## 2

# THE OPENING MOVE

Having the opening move is an advantage; knowing how to play it can be crucial.

We will begin this chapter with a table of recommended opening moves for all rolls.

You might think that there should be a standard best opening move for any throw of the dice. But for many throws (contrary to some other books on backgammon) there just isn't a clearcut standard, any more than there is a standard first move at chess.

You will note that some moves in the table are marked with one or two asterisks. Where no asterisk appears it means that the recommended play is greatly superior to any other. One asterisk means that some other plays are almost as good. Two asterisks indicate that there is an alternate move that is just about as good. Following the table we will explain why we recommend our plays and will discuss the various interesting alternative moves.

You will of course grasp the instructions in this chapter and those that follow more quickly and easily of you have set up an actual backgammon board (see Diagram 1) and work out each move on it as we go along. Remember throughout that you are white and move first.

### TABLE OF OPENING MOVES

6–5     Move one back man from black one point to black
        twelve point.

6–4*    Move a back man from black one point to black
        eleven point.

6–3**     Move one man from black one point to black bar point, and one from black twelve point to your own ten point.

6–2**     Move a back man from black one point to black bar point, and a man from black twelve point to your eleven point.

6–1     Make your bar point (move one man from black twelve point and one from your own eight point to your bar point).

5–4     Move two men from black twelve point to your eight and nine points.

5–3**     Make your three point (move one man from your eight point and one from your six point to your three point).

5–2     Move two men from black twelve point to your eight and eleven points.

5–1*     Move one man from black twelve point to your eight point, and one back man from black one to black two point.

4–3     Move two men from black twelve point to your nine and ten points.

4–2     Make your four point (move one man from your eight point and one from your six point to your four point).

4–1*     Move one man from black twelve point to your nine point, and one back man from black one to black two point.

3–2*     Move two men from black twelve point to your ten and eleven points.

3–1     Make your five point (move one man from your

eight point and one man from your six point to your five point).

2–1*   Move one man from black twelve point to your eleven point, and one back man from black one to black two point.

TABLE OF OPENING MOVES FOR DOUBLETS
(Some people play that you may start with one)

Double 6   Make both bar points (i.e., move two men from black one point to black bar point and two men from black twelve point to your bar point).

Double 5   Move two men from black twelve point to your three point.

Double 4**  Move your two back men from black one point to black five point, and two men from black twelve to your own nine point.

Double 3*  Make your own five and three points (move two men from your eight point to your five point, and two men from your six point to your three point).

Double 2*  Make your eleven and four points (move two men from black twelve point to your eleven point, and two men from your six point to your four point).

Double 1   Make your bar and five points (move two men from your eight point to your bar point, and two men from your six point to your five point).

## Discussion

Remember, when *no* asterisk appears, it means that the recommended play is so outstanding that there is no need to consider any other. *One* asterisk means that there is at least one other play that should be considered; *two* asterisks indicate that an alternate move is *just about as good* as the play we recommend in the table.

Now for the individual plays: *

[2] *Double 6. Make both bar points.* This play takes full advantage of the twenty-four points that this powerful throw permits you to move, cramps your opponent's back men (since making your own bar point gives you a three-point block), and gets your back men to a strategic spot. The only weakness of the position is that you have advanced very fast, and those two men on your opponent's

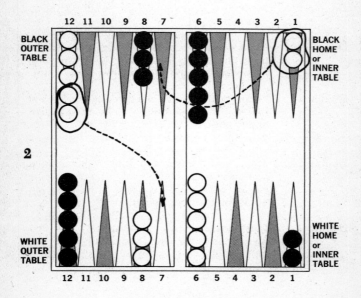

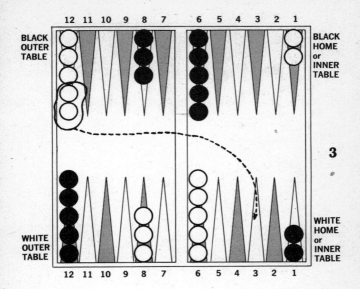

bar point must be moved some time or other, which may force you to leave a blot when you don't want to. But it is an excellent roll, and can give you a great advantage in a "running game," which we'll discuss in Chapter 5.

[3] *Double 5. Move two men from black twelve point to your three point.* This is the only opening doublet that is a poor roll. The recommended play offers little advantage, but is the only safe way to play double 5.

[4] *Double 4\* \*. Move your two back men from black one point to black five point, and two men from black twelve to your own nine point.* We have marked double 4 with two asterisks because moving two men from black twelve to your own five point is just about as good as the play we recommend. Our recommended play gives you great mobility: Your back men are brought forward to where they aim directly at the black outer board and indirectly at your own outer board, while covering one of

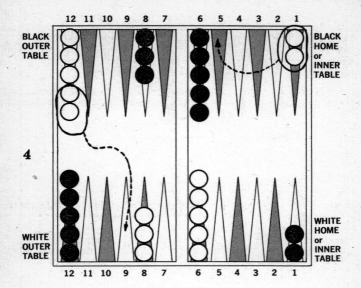

the most important points in your opponent's inner board; your two men on your nine point threaten the bar, the five, the four, and the three points.

The alternate play leaves you with your five point made immediately, and the more you play backgammon the more you will see the great value of this point.

It has been said that there is no bad way to play double 4. This is an exaggeration. As a hideous example, you could move four men from your six point to your two point! But there *are* two other fairly good ways to play this move.

One is to make your four and two points (by moving two men from your eight point to your four point, and two men from your six point to your two point). This gives you three points made in your inner board—but one of them is the two point, which you needn't be in any great hurry to make. You should much prefer to go after

34

your higher-numbered points, since they are far more important points in blocking your opponent's back men. Your two men on the two point can never be used to work on either the three or the five point.

The other move is to bring your two back men out to the black nine point. This starts to make the play into a running game.

These last two plays are reasonable, but definitely inferior to either of the two we recommend.

[5] *Double 3\**. *Make your own five and three points.* Double 3 is another roll that is hard to play badly. We have given only one asterisk to our recommended play because it is extremely strong: it takes you a long way toward blocking your opponent's back men.

However, making your own bar point (by moving two men from black twelve point) is almost as good; and there are all sorts of strong combination plays, such as

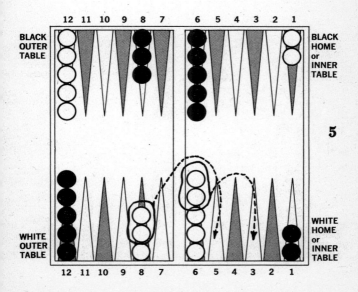

**5**

moving your two back men from black one point to black four point and making your own five point with two men from your eight point.

[6] *Double 2°. Make your eleven and four points.* The alternate play would be to move your back men up from black one to black five point. This would be fine for defense, but why start the game with defense when you can make a strong attacking play? Our recommendation is a good blocking play, and it affords you a good chance of making an additional blocking point on your next roll.

[7] *Double 1. Make your bar and five points.* This is just about as powerful a move as the one we recommend for double 3, for the same reason: blocking your opponent's back men. You immediately establish a three-point consecutive block, and need only a 5 on your next roll to establish a four-point block (by moving a man from black twelve point to your own eight point).

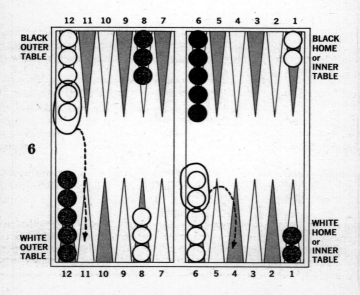

[8] *6–5. Move one back man from black one point to black twelve point.* This move is so obvious that virtually no explanation is needed: you have gotten one of your back men halfway home *safely,* and are off to a strong running game.

In backgammon circles the move is sometimes called "lover's leap."

*6–4\*, 6–3\*\*, 6–2\*\*.* These three rolls should be considered together. There is no way to play one of these rolls intelligently without exposing a man to a direct shot (a "direct" shot is one in which it is necessary to move the number on only one die in order to hit a blot; a "combination" shot requires both moves—that is, the total of both dice—in order to hit the blot).

The old-fashioned play with all three of them was to run, using the full throw to bring one of the two back men out into the black outer board. Should this man be

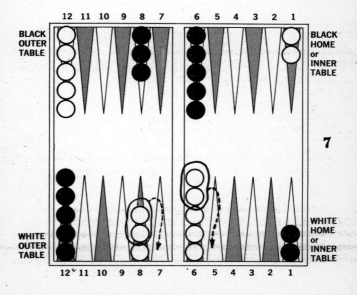

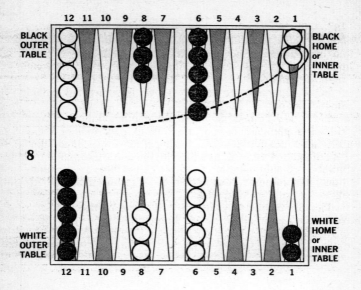

hit, you would only have lost your first roll; should he not be hit you would have him well-positioned to move into your outer board on your second throw.

The modern play is to use the six to move one back man to the black bar point, and to move a man from the black twelve point into your own outer board. The man on the black bar point is exposed to a direct 6 or 1 plus some combination shots. The odds are two to one that he will be hit. But unless he is hit by a point-making roll (in this case 6–1; double 6; double 3; or double 1) you will have a lot of possible return shots against your opponent's vulnerable blot, and you have lost little anyway. If your man is not hit, your position is highly advantageous.

[9]6–4°. *Move a back man from black one point to black eleven point.* You'll note that we recommend the traditional play for 6–4; we regard the modern play as inferior for two reasons. The first is that with our recommended

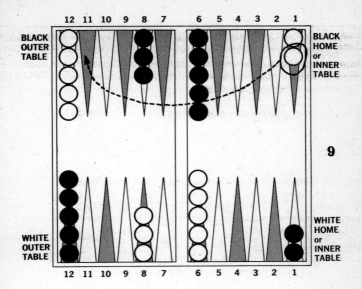

running play, your blot is exposed to only a direct 2 (from one of your opponent's men on your twelve point). The actual probability of his rolling this is eleven out of thirty-six possible shots. The second reason is that if you moved a man four points from the black twelve point in the modern manner, he would be on your nine point, exposed to a hit by one of your opponent's back men should he throw any 8, one of the likeliest throws.

A word of warning: don't be tempted to use an opening 6–4 to make your two point (by moving one man from your eight point and one from your six point). A point made in your board is always valuable, but the ones to aim for first are the five and four points: not only do they impede the movement of your opponent's back men but they also furnish good landing places for your men as you start to make lower-numbered points later on in the game. Men on the two point, however, are almost entirely

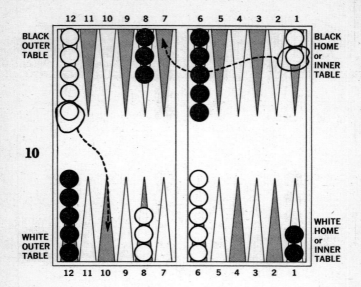

out of play since their only possible move is to the one point.

[10] *6–3\* \**. *Move one man from black one point to black bar point, and one from black twelve point to your own ten point.* We recommend this modern play, but with two asterisks to show that the old play is just about as good (one man from black one point to black ten point). But not quite: when you run all the way with 6–3 your blot is exposed to a direct 3 and a 2–1 from one of black's men on your twelve point; such vulnerability makes this play slightly less desirable than our recommended play.

[11] *6–2\* \**. *Move a back man from black one point to black bar point, and a man from black twelve point to your eleven point.* We have two asterisks after this recommendation also, but the alternative we suggest is not the old-fashioned running play. It is yet a *third* play: move a man from the black twelve point to your own five point.

40

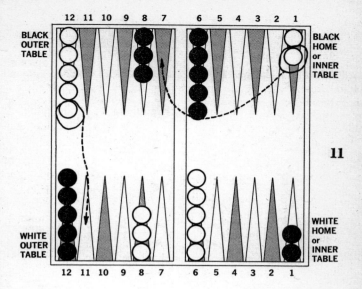

If he is hit, you won't like it, but if he survives, you have made a start toward securing that most valuable point.

With a 6–2 opening throw we don't like the running play at all (one man from black one point to black nine point) since it exposes your blot to a straight 4 or 3–1 or double 2 (a total of fourteen possible shots).

[12] 6–1. *Make your bar point.* One of the best opening rolls. You make your bar point and have a powerful block of three points in a row: your six, bar, and eight points.

[13] 5–4. *Move two men from black twelve point to your eight and nine points.* Let's look at the recommended play first. You expose a blot on your nine point. Your opponent will hit that blot with one of his back men if he rolls 6–2, 5–3, or double 4. This will put three of your men back in black's home board instead of two, but that is nothing to worry about so early in the game; you would be at only a slight disadvantage. (He could also hit your blot with one

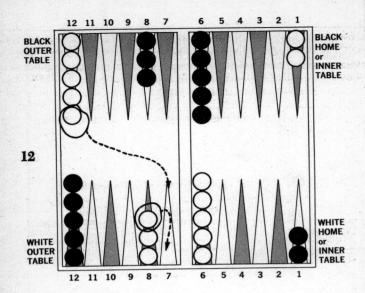

of his back men if he rolls double 2, but his gain from such a move is so inconsequential that he would be foolish not to make his normal play with that fine roll.)

If he rolls any of the other thirty possible rolls, he won't be able to touch your blot, and that blot will become a source of strength. It gives you an extra man bearing on your bar point and on the good points in your inner board, greatly increasing your chances of making one of those points; and if you roll a 4 next, you can cover that man with one of your men on black twelve, thereby securing your nine point. Furthermore that extra man on your eight point will often prove useful later in the game.

There are two inferior plays. The first is to move one man from black twelve point to your eight point, and one back man to black five point. This is superficially attractive, but experience has shown that it is generally inadvisable to move *one* man to your opponent's five point *on*

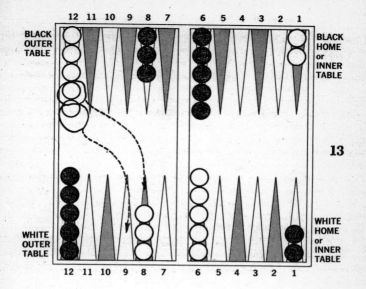

*your first turn.* If he rolls some number that enables him to make the five point, he will do so at great profit. If one of the numbers he rolls is 3 or 1, he is likely to hit you even if he exposes a blot. You will of course have plenty of chances to hit him back, but will gain little. If you don't hit him back, he will be ready to make that point.

The other play is to bring a back man all the way to the black ten point. That man will then be exposed to a direct 3 or 2–1. You won't lose much if he is hit, but you won't gain much if he is missed either.

[14] 5–3* *. *Make your three point.* There is a strong alternate play that is becoming more and more popular in expert circles. It is simply to move two men from the black twelve point to your eight and ten points. It means taking chances early in the game but greatly increases your chance to make the bar, five, or four point at your next roll, and the modern theory is that the three point does

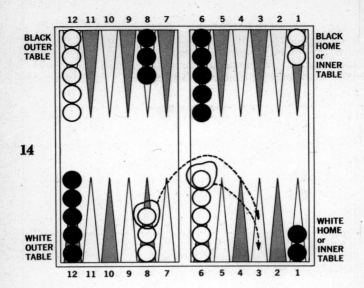

not really become valuable until after you have managed to make the four or five point.

We have marked our recommended play with two asterisks because we consider this more aggressive alternate just about as good.

[15] 5–2. *Move two men from black twelve point to your eight and eleven points.* This is by far the best play because you begin to set up a strong blocking action in relative safety. There are two weaker plays. The first is to move one man from the black twelve point to your own six point. This play risks nothing, but it gains nothing either: you are safe, but you haven't done anything to better your position. It is possible to make the same silly, safe play with 4–3, or a similar silly, safe play to your eight point with 4–1 or 3–2, and we will dispose of all of these right now by pointing out that the man who sits quietly never falls down but also never gets anywhere.

A really bad play with 5–2 is to use the 2 to split your

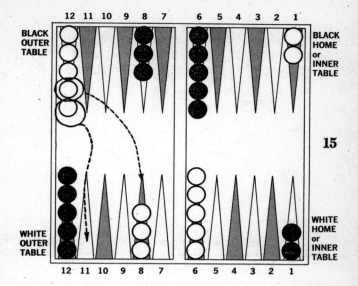

BLACK OUTER TABLE

BLACK HOME or INNER TABLE

WHITE OUTER TABLE

WHITE HOME or INNER TABLE

15

back men by moving one of them to the black three point. The split to the one and three points in the black board is the worst split you can have, for one important reason. If your opponent rolls double 5, he makes both his one and three points and puts both your men on the bar. In a gambling game, unless you can then bring them both in immediately your opponent will have a strong enough position to end the game by doubling you.

[16] *5–1°. Move one man from black twelve point to your eight point, and one back man from black one to black two point.* With 5–1 we *do* recommend splitting your two back men, but that split to the black two point is quite good. Your opponent can hit both your men with 4–1, but this doesn't represent much gain for him. To begin with, you might then roll some combination with a 1 and send his blot all the way back to the bar. If you don't roll a 1, that man he has placed on his one point will be out of play for the rest of the game. If he proceeds to cover it, he will

45

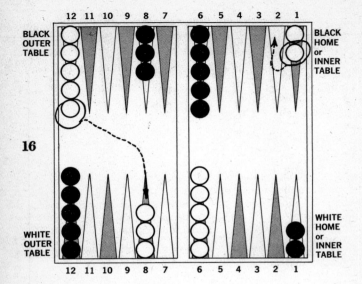

have a second man out of play. Good players do make their one point on occasion, but they prefer not to do so until they have made at least one higher point.

If, instead of 4–1, your opponent happens to roll 6–4, he will be able to hit your blot on his two point and secure that point; but this also represents little real gain, and there are better plays on the board for his 6–4. As we have said, at this early stage of play the two point is worth very little to him.

If he fails to hit either of your men on his one and two points, you will be in position to make one of the advanced points in his board, or his bar point, with one of several rolls. In addition, you will have doubled your coverage of the black outer board, so that if he chooses to move a blot into that terrain, you are twice as likely to be able to hit it.

There are two other plays with 5–1 that have achieved some popularity and have a good deal to recommend them. One is to move a back man right to the black bar point. It's an interesting gambit—you have lost little if your opponent takes the bait and hits that blot, and moreover you have a very good chance of hitting him back when coming in off the bar.

The other play is to use the 5 to move from black twelve to your eight point, but use the 1 to move a man from your six to your five point. You lose a good deal if that blot is hit, but you gain a lot if it is missed.

[17] *4–3. Move two men from black twelve point to your nine and ten points.* You leave two blots, but your opponent can't hit both of them. If neither is hit they are in excellent position to help you build your bar point, five point, or four point; or you may be able to cover one, giving you possession of your nine or ten point.

Alternative plays are to split your back men and just move one man from black twelve into your outer board. The better split is to move a back man three to the black four point, rather than to move four to the black five point as some strategists advise.

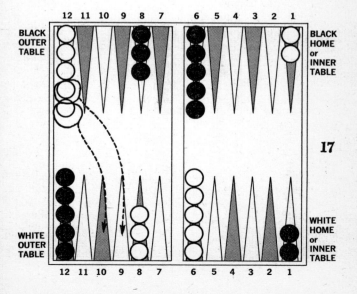

BLACK OUTER TABLE

BLACK HOME or INNER TABLE

WHITE OUTER TABLE

WHITE HOME or INNER TABLE

17

A very old-fashioned play is to move both back men up. Don't make this play against an opponent who knows enough to hit one of those blots if he can do so. You may come out all right, but it is more likely that your game will go sour immediately. (Also see discussion under 5–2.)

[18] *4–2. Make your four point.* This is a good roll, and no discussion of alternates is necessary. Your four point is very valuable, obviously, and any other play will expose a blot needlessly.

[19] *4–1.° Move one man from black twelve point to your nine point, and one back man from black one to black two point.* This is not a good roll of the dice, and our recommended play has its risks, as you know from previous discussion. The good alternate play with 4–1 is to move one man to your nine point and the other man to your five point. This is wonderful when it works—that is, if black doesn't hit one of your blots, and if you can cover them on the next roll. The trouble is that your blot on the

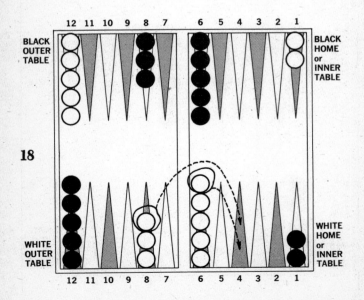

48

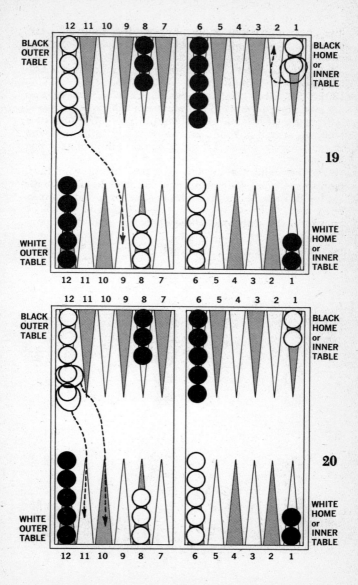

BLACK OUTER TABLE

BLACK HOME or INNER TABLE

WHITE OUTER TABLE

WHITE HOME or INNER TABLE

12 11 10 9 8 7    6 5 4 3 2 1

BLACK OUTER TABLE

BLACK HOME or INNER TABLE

WHITE OUTER TABLE

WHITE HOME or INNER TABLE

12 11 10 9 8 7    6 5 4 3 2 1

five point is exposed to any 4, plus 3–1, double 2, and double 1, while your other blot is exposed to 6–2, 5–3, double 4, and double 2. In addition, double 4 and double 2 hit *both* your blots. This represents too much risk. (Also see discussion under 5–2.)

[20] 3–2*. *Move two men from black twelve point to your ten and eleven points.* The recommended move with 3–2 puts two men in your outer board, a good start toward a blocking strategy. Your blots are exposed to only a nine or ten, and you are in a fine position to make points if you are not hit.

The best alternate play is to move one of your back men to the black four point, and one man from the black twelve to your eleven point. A poor play is to move a man from the black twelve to your ten point and one back man from the black one to the black three point. Remem-

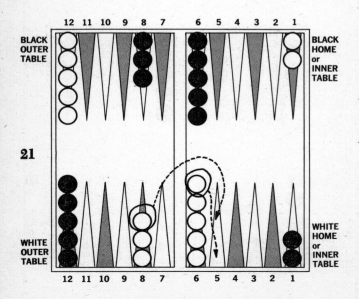

50

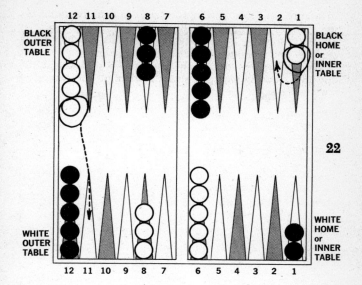

ber, the least desirable split of your two back men is to the black one and three points, where double 5 will enable your opponent to hit them both. (Also see discussion under 5–2.)

[21] *3–1. Make your five point.* There is no need to comment on the play of 3–1. When you are not allowed to start with a doublet, it is your best first roll; you have made the most important point on your home board, and created an additional block against your opponent.

[22] *2–1\*. Move one man from black twelve point to your eleven point, and one back man from black one to black two point.* Our recommended play moves one man into your outer board with relative safety, and splits your two back men in the most effective manner, as we have discussed.

The slightly inferior play is to move from the black twelve

to your eleven point and from your six to your five point. As we remarked under 4–1, the man on your five point is exposed to any 4, 3–1, double 2, or double 1; while a 6–4 enables your opponent to hit both your blots.

We can't stress too much the need to understand the opening move before going any further in your study of backgammon.

3

# THE REPLY TO THE OPENING MOVE

Throughout this chapter our analysis of various plays will always refer back to the previous chapter's discussion of opening moves. The reply is also a first move, but of course the way your opponent has already moved will help determine your play. He may have blocked some move you would otherwise make, he may have given you some extra option, or he may have changed the relative value of different plays.

In general:

1. *If he has made a point in his inner board, with 3–1, 4–2, or 5–3, you don't want to move a back man to his bar point.* Thus, you do not consider such a move with 6–4, 6–3, or 6–2, as you would if yours were the opening move (refer here, as throughout, to our discussion of these moves in Chapter 2). The reason for this is that you would be getting into a game where the odds are against you:

As we explained in Chapter 2's discussion of 6–4, 6–3, and 6–2, you expect to be hit when you leave a blot on your opponent's bar point. You hope to hit him back and to initiate what we call a "blot-hitting contest." However, in this case you would be entering such a contest with a distinct handicap. You have what is known as a "one-point board," since the only point you hold in your inner board is the six point you began with. But your opponent has already made an extra point in his inner board, giving him a two-point board, so if he hits your blot on his bar point, the odds are only eight to one in favor of your bringing a man back in from the bar on your next roll. But if you did manage to enter and then to hit back *his* blot, the odds are thirty-five to one in favor of his coming in from the bar on his next roll. Eight-to-one odds in your favor may look pretty good, but they are not nearly as good as the thirty-five-to-one odds in *his* favor—and though the result of a blot-hitting contest is usually close to a draw, *any player who fails to enter at any roll is likely to find himself losing the game*. That extra point your opponent holds in his inner board cramps your style; you have only four points on which to enter your man from the bar, and your full play is restricted. If he should then make a *third* point in his inner board, the odds in favor of your entering go way down to only three to one, while if you manage to make a second point in your own inner board, all you will have done is get back on equal terms with him.

2. *If he has split his back men, don't expose a man in your outer board;* that man will be vulnerable to attack by both of those back men.

3. *If he has put a blot where you can hit it, in general you want to hit it.*

It is impossible to go over every combination of first and second rolls, but we can show you how you should reply to a few typical first moves. Master these thoroughly; they'll help you play all other combinations more skillfully, too.

*Reply to 6–1.* In Diagram 23 black has rolled 6–1 and made his bar point. This makes it impossible for you to move a 6 with one of your back men, so you cannot play double 6 or 6–5 the way you would if he had not made that bar point. Instead of being good rolls, they both become unsatisfactory and should be played as follows:

*Double 6.* Move four men from black twelve point to your bar point. This leaves a blot but is the best you can do.

*6–5.* Move one man from his twelve point to your bar point and another to your eight point. The man on your bar point will be a blot, but there is no way to avoid leaving a blot somewhere; in such instances you should *leave your blot where it will be of most use to you if not hit.*

Most other replies to 6–1 are played as if they were opening moves. The exceptions are:

*Double 3.* Make your five point (move two men from

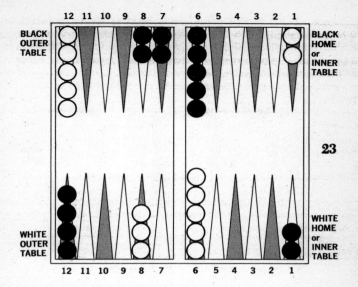

your eight point), and move your two back men on the black one point up to the black four point. Your opponent has started to hem in your back men by making his bar point; your play counters his move.

*Double 2.* Either move those two back men up to the black five point, or move them to the black three point and make your four point (by moving two men from your six point).

5–4. Run all the way to black ten with one of your two back men, again because your opponent is starting to hem them in. Try to get one out before he hems them in any more.

4–3. Move one man from his twelve point to your nine point, and one of your back men to his four point. Again, you want to start to do something with those back men before he blocks them further.

3–2. Use the same move as for 4–3, except that your

man on his twelve point moves to your eleven point. As you'll recall, these last two plays were given as alternates in our discussion of them as first moves. The change in adverse position has made them first instead of second choices here.

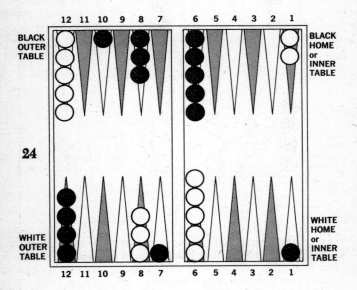

*Reply to our recommended 6–3 move.* In Diagram 24 black has started with 6–3, and has moved one man from your one point to your bar point and one from your twelve point to his ten point:

*Doubles.* If in reply you roll any double, you should make you regular first move (or, in the case of double 4, one of two possible moves; see the discussion of opening moves in Chapter 2), except with double 3. With double 3, you simply move two men from black twelve point to your bar point in order to hit his blot.

Note that our recommended opening plays for double 6 and double 1 become even stronger here than as opening moves, since you hit a blot in addition to making your points.

*6–5.* This becomes a very strong roll, so valuable that you do not play the normal opening move for 6–5. You should use the 6 to hit his man on your bar point with one of your men on his twelve point, and use the 5 to hit his man on your one point with one of yours on your six point. This leaves him with two men on the bar (and, in a gambling game, with a potential quick loss).

*6–4.* Use the 6 to hit his blot on your bar point with one of your men on the black twelve point. Move a back man to black five point with the 4. Do *not* make your own two point.

*6–3.* Hit the blot on his ten point with one of your back men.

*6–2.* Hit his blot on your bar point with one of your men on his twelve point, and move another man from his twelve point to your eleven point. If he does not come in off the bar and hit you, you are in an excellent position to make any of several good points, setting up a strong block to his back men.

*6–1.* Make your bar point, as you would for an opening move. This good move has become even better, since you hit his blot while making that key point.

*5–4.* Hit the blot on his ten point with one of your back men (playing the 4 first, of course).

*5–3.* Make your three point. You cannot hit your opponent, so you may as well make a potentially valuable point on your inner board.

*5–2.* This is always a poor throw, but black's man at your bar point has even ruined your normal play. We recommend that you move a man from black twelve point to your eight point and a man from your six to your four point. This is in line with the general principle that if you have to expose a blot to a direct shot, expose one where it will help you most if your blot isn't hit.

*5–1.* Use the 1 to hit his blot on your bar point and the 5 to hit his blot on your one point (see play for 6–5).

*4–3.* The best you can do here is to move a man from his twelve point to your six point. You will expose two blots with any other move (this is one of the few times you should play safe at the start of the game).

*4–2.* This play offers alternate choices of equal merit. You might ignore his blot and just make your four point (moving a man each from your eight and six points); or you might move the whole six points with one of the men on his twelve point in order to hit that blot on your bar point. It is one of the many, many situations in backgammon where there is just no best way to play a certain roll.

*4–1.* Hit his blot on your bar point with one of the men on your eight point, and move a back man to his five point.

*3–2.* All you can do is to play safe by moving a man from the black twelve point to your eight point.

*3–1.* Ignore the temptation to hit that blot on your bar point, and just make your five point by moving a man each from your eight and six points. (Remember that the man you move from your eight point to your five point passes over your opponent's blot but does not send it back home; you must touch down on the exact point a blot is on in order to hit it.)

*2–1.* Hit his blot on your bar point, and move a man from his twelve point to your eleven point.

*Reply to the running move for 6–3.* In Diagram 25 black has played his opening 6–3 by running all the way with a back man to your ten point:

You play *double 6, double 4, double 2, double 1, 6–5, 4–2, 6–1, 5–1,* or *4–1* as you would play an opening roll.

*Double 5.* Move two men each from your eight and six points, making your three and one points. You hit his blot on your one point as you do this. In general, you should play double 5 this way any time that you can "point on a blot" (hit a blot and make that point in the same throw).

*Double 3* becomes even better than normal. Move two men from the black twelve point and hit his blot on your ten point; then either move two men from your eight point to make your five point, or advance your two back men to the black four point.

*6–4.* You should not make the normal running play with a back man, since your blot on black's eleven point would be exposed to direct hits by either a 2 or 4. Instead, use our recommended alternate play for the opening move: move one back man to the black bar point, and one man "around the corner," from black twelve to your nine point.

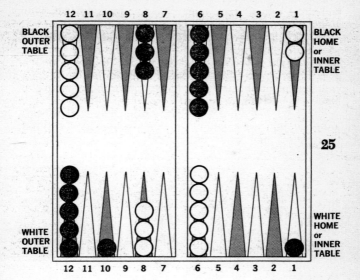

*6–3, 5–3, 4–3, 3–2,* or *2–1.* With all of these moves, you should use the 3 to hit his blot on your ten point. With 6–3, use the 6 to move a back man to the black bar point. With 5–3, 4–3, or 3–2, you should use the 5, 4, or 2 to move another man around the corner from the black twelve point. With 2–1, of course, it takes your whole move to hit the blot on your ten point.

*6–2.* You can't afford *either* to run with a back man to the black nine point, *or* to move a man to his bar point and another to your eleven point, because you can be hit too easily. Instead, you should move a man all the way from his twelve point to your own five point. Once more, you are exposing a blot where you stand to gain a lot if it isn't hit.

*5–2.* That man on your ten point spoils your normal play since if you put a blot on your eleven point it will be exposed to any 1, in addition to 6–4. The best you can do is to move a man from his twelve point to your eight point, and drop a man from your six point down to your four point.

*3–1.* There is no objection to making your five point as you would if it were the first play of the game, but we have a slight preference for the following play. Use the 3 to move a man from his twelve point to hit the blot on your ten point and the 1 to move one of the men on the black one point to the two point.

*Reply to 3–1.* In Diagram 26 black has started with 3–1, making his five point. You will see how good this roll is as we examine your possible replies.

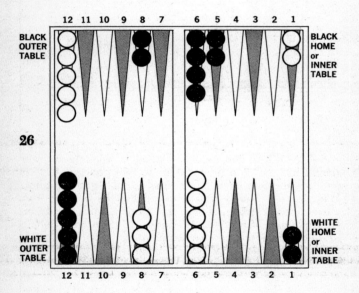

Make your normal opening plays unless you roll the following:

*Double 4.* You can't move your back men. Your best play is to bring two men from his twelve point to your five point.

*Double 3.* Make your five point with two men from

your eight point, and move your two back men up to your opponent's four point.

*Double 2.* Make your four point with two men from your six point, and move your back men up to his three point. This play, like our recommended play for double 3, gets the back men on their way out of trouble.

*6–4, 6–3, 6–2.* When you roll any of these, use the full roll to run with one of your back men. Do not consider splitting the move and leaving one man on his bar point. As we explained at the beginning of this chapter, the last thing you want to do is to get into a blot-hitting contest when your opponent has two points made in his inner board and you have only one in yours.

*4–3, 3–2.* Move two men from black twelve point. When your opponent has made his five point, you *don't* want to use the 3 to advance a back man to his four point. If he hits this blot you are likely to be in serious trouble.

Master all of these moves and the logic behind each; they will help you reply to *any* opening move with greater skill.

When you have done that, you'll be ready for your first look at Basic Probability.

# 4

# BASIC PROBABILITY

When players are evenly matched, backgammon is essentially a game of probability. Theoretically, you could then take a computer and work out your mathematical chances in any position. Practically, however, there are so many factors involved—including the kind of game your opponent plays—that even the world's largest and most sophisticated computer would be unable to handle this problem, except perhaps in the very late stages of the game. Experience will teach you that in some situations and against some kinds of players you may be wise to forget about the odds and concentrate on your opponent's strategy. But in the long run the more you know how to figure the odds, the better the game you'll play.

A word of warning: don't expect to assimilate everything in this chapter the first, second, or even the third time you read it. Go through it carefully now, and then go on to the next chapter—but *get in the habit of referring back to it often as you read the rest of the book.* You'll learn how to figure the odds more and more quickly and easily, and many key principles will eventually become second nature to you.

Now let's see what there is to learn, *without* the use of a computer. As a starter here are the thirty-six rolls possible with two dice.

### TABLE 1
#### COMBINATIONS OF THE DICE

| | |
|---|---|
| Double 1 | 1 |
| Double 2 | 1 |
| Double 3 | 1 |

```
Double  4 . . . . . . . . . . . . . . . . . . . . . .1
Double  5 . . . . . . . . . . . . . . . . . . . . . .1
Double  6 . . . . . . . . . . . . . . . . . . . . . .1
1 and 2, or 2 and 1 . . . . . . . . . . . .2
1 and 3, or 3 and 1 . . . . . . . . . . . .2
1 and 4, or 4 and 1 . . . . . . . . . . . .2
1 and 5, or 5 and 1 . . . . . . . . . . . .2
1 and 6, or 6 and 1 . . . . . . . . . . . .2
2 and 3, or 3 and 2 . . . . . . . . . . . .2
2 and 4, or 4 and 2 . . . . . . . . . . . .2
2 and 5, or 5 and 2 . . . . . . . . . . . .2
2 and 6, or 6 and 2 . . . . . . . . . . . .2
3 and 4, or 4 and 3 . . . . . . . . . . . .2
3 and 5, or 5 and 3 . . . . . . . . . . . .2
3 and 6, or 6 and 3 . . . . . . . . . . . .2
4 and 5, or 5 and 4 . . . . . . . . . . . .2
4 and 6, or 6 and 4 . . . . . . . . . . . .2
5 and 6, or 6 and 5 . . . . . . . . . . . .2
                                    ___
                                    36
```

Notice that a double counts as one roll only, while a number such as 6–5 occurs as two dice combinations. Although 6–5 and 5–6 look alike when rolled, they are actually two different rolls. This difference becomes obvious if you are rolling dice of different colors, say one red die and one green die.

Looking at Table 1, you can see that there are eleven ways to roll a specific number, such as 1. Are there, then, twenty-two ways to roll one of two numbers, such as 1 or 2? You might think so, but that isn't the case. There are only twenty ways, since 1–2 and 2–1 cannot be counted twice.

Similarly, there are twenty-seven ways to roll one of three specified numbers, thirty-two ways to roll one of four, and thirty-five ways to roll one of five.

Table 2 merely reflects the preceding, since the "number of points open" corresponds to the number of different numbers you can roll. Thus if you have a man on the bar and there are five points open in your opponent's inner board, you want to know the probability of rolling any of five specified numbers.

It is also useful, when you have to leave a blot some-

## TABLE 2
### PROBABILITY OF ENTERING FROM THE BAR

| Number of points open | Ways to come in | Chance of coming in | Odds in favor or against |
|---|---|---|---|
| 5 | 35 | 97% | 35 to 1 in favor |
| 4 | 32 | 89% | 8 to 1 in favor |
| 3 | 27 | 75% | 3 to 1 in favor |
| 2 | 20 | 56% | 5 to 4 in favor |
| 1 | 11 | 31% | 25 to 11 against |

where, to be able to count the number of rolls that will hit you. When exposing a man to a *single shot, the closer you are to your opponent's threat, the less chance that you will be hit*. Thus if exposed to a 1 (an enemy man one point away), there are only eleven ways to be hit, since only a 1 hits you. When you are exposed to a 2, you can hit in twelve ways: eleven 2s plus double 1.

When a combination or *double shot* (i.e., more than 6) is necessary to hit you, with one minor exception, *the farther away you are the less the chance that you will be hit*. It is not difficult to work these chances out by counting, but as a matter of convenience they are listed in Table 3 for all distances from one to twelve.

## TABLE 3
### PROBABILITY OF HITTING A BLOT
(This table takes for granted no enemy points between you and the blot.)

| Distance away | Ways to be hit | Chances of being hit | Odds against being hit |
|---|---|---|---|
| 1 | 11 | 31% | 25 to 11 |
| 2 | 12 | 33% | 2 to 1 |
| 3 | 14 | 39% | 11 to 7 |
| 4 | 15 | 42% | 7 to 5 |
| 5 | 15 | 42% | 7 to 5 |
| 6 | 17 | 47% | 19 to 17 |

| 7  | 6 | 17% | 5 to 1   |
| 8  | 6 | 17% | 5 to 1   |
| 9  | 5 | 14% | 31 to 5  |
| 10 | 3 | 8%  | 11 to 1  |
| 11 | 2 | 6%  | 17 to 1  |
| 12 | 3 | 8%  | 11 to 1  |

You may also be hit by double 4 when sixteen away, by double 5 when fifteen or twenty away, and by double 6 when eighteen or twenty-four away (each of these is, of course, only one out of thirty-six possible shots, or odds of thirty-five to one against being hit).

When you hold one or more points between your blot and your opponent's threatening man, the number of ways you can be hit is reduced. Thus if you hold your two, five, and six points and expose a blot on your bar point to an enemy man on your one point, he can hit you with any 6 or with 4–2 or double 3, but he cannot hit you with 5–1 or double 2, so you are exposed to fourteen rolls instead of seventeen.

When you are exposed to two numbers, the chance that you will be hit is determined by *adding the two individual ways together and subtracting duplications*. Thus if you are exposed to men six and one points away, you can be hit in twenty-four ways: seventeen ways from the 6, plus eleven ways from the 1, minus the four ways for 6–1 and 5–1, which hit you from either spot. This same total can be arrived at another way: there are eleven direct 6s, plus nine direct 1s that do not include a 6, plus 4–2, 2–4, double 3, and double 2—still the same twenty-four ways.

You can also check large probabilities of being hit by counting the rolls that miss. Thus, if you are exposed to 6 and 1, the only shots that miss are double 5, double 4, 5–4, 5–3, 5–2, 4–3, and 3–2, for a total of twelve rolls; thirty-six minus twelve gives you the same twenty-four ways.

Make a habit of counting the number of rolls that can hit you when you must expose a blot. There are some unusual figures here. After arriving at the position shown in Diagram 27, you double and proceed to roll a 3–2. You

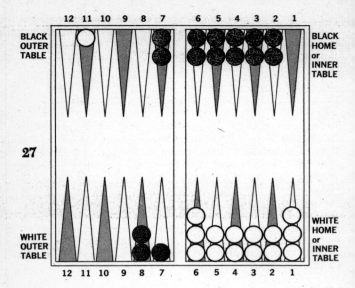

27

complain a little to the gods that plague backgammon players, and then settle down to make your best play. You can move your blot five, three, two, or no points, but you can't bring him to safety.

You don't have to count to see that you should either move him all the way or not at all; moving him three or two exposes him to far too many possible hits. At first glance you would expect to be in less danger where you are since you are exposed to only one direct shot, but you are better off moving all the way up to your nine point. There are seventeen ways to shoot a 6, plus four ways to shoot 5–2 and 4–3, or twenty-one total ways you can be hit where you are by one of black's men on your seven or eight point. But there are only twenty ways to hit you with a 2 or 1 if you move up.

Furthermore, there is another reason for you to move up. Once you do so, if you are not hit right away you are going to be home free on your next roll (barring double 1).

If you stay where you are, double 3, double 6, or any roll that totals six or less will still leave you in trouble (and there are thirteen such rolls).

Now look at the position shown in Diagram 28. You roll 6–1. You have to move 6 from black's nine point; your problem is the 1. If you move your blot to black's ten point, you leave only fourteen rolls instead of fifteen to hit you, but the correct play is to stay exposed on the nine point.

The reason is that here you are really worried about the rolls that will allow your opponent to hit your blot *and at the same time to cover his own blot in his inner board*. If you move up, he can hit you and cover his blot with five rolls (double 3, 3–4, and 3–6). If you stop on the ten point, he can hit you and cover with only four rolls (double 2, double 4, and 4–5).

Let's see why you are so worried about the hit-and-cover combination. The reason is that if he hits you and fails to cover, you have twenty ways (see Table 2) to

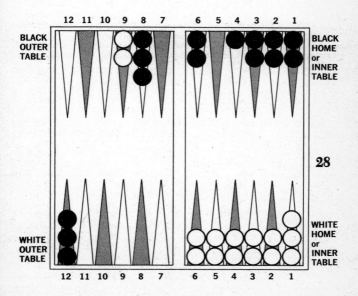

BLACK OUTER TABLE

BLACK HOME or INNER TABLE

28

WHITE OUTER TABLE

WHITE HOME or INNER TABLE

12 11 10 9 8 7 6 5 4 3 2 1

come right in, and eleven of these twenty ways allow you to come in and hit his blot. If he hits you and covers, you have only eleven ways to come in at all. If you don't come in immediately, you will be doubled (if it is a gambling game or tournament play) and you would have to concede the game right away. The rules don't compel you to refuse that double, but if you are playing for anything of value you really can't afford to take it.

Table 4 lists the probability of bearing off your last one or two men in one or two rolls, in all combinations. Mastering it is essential in order to know how to move your men at the very end of the game, and in considering late double and redoubles:

TABLE 4

PROBABILITY OF GETTING THE LAST ONE OR TWO MEN OFF
IN ONE OF TWO ROLLS

| Total points to go | Points on which your man or men are located | In one roll you have the Number of winning rolls | In one roll you have the following: Probability of winning | In two rolls you have the following: Probability of winning |
|---|---|---|---|---|
| 12 | 6–6 | 4 | 11% | 78% |
| 11 | 6–5 | 6 | 17% | 88% |
| 10 | 5–5 | 6 | 17% | 92% |
|  | 6–4 | 8 | 22% | 93% |
| 9 | 5–4 | 10 | 28% | 96% |
|  | 6–3 | 10 | 28% | 97% |
| 8 | 4–4 | 11 | 31% | 98% |
|  | 6–2 | 13 | 36% | 99% |
|  | 5–3 | 14 | 39% | 99% |
| 7 | 6–1 | 15 | 42% | 99+% |
|  | 4–3 | 17 | 47% | 99+% |
|  | 5–2 | 19 | 53% | 99+% |
| 6 | 3–3 | 17 | 47% | 100% |
|  | 5–1 or 4–2 | 23 | 64% | 100% |
|  | 6 | 27 | 75% | 100% |
| 5 | 3–2 | 25 | 69% | 100% |
|  | 4–1 | 29 | 81% | 100% |
|  | 5 | 31 | 86% | 100% |
| 4 | 2–2 | 26 | 72% | 100% |
|  | 3–1 or 4 | 34 | 94% | 100% |
| 3 | 2–1 or 3 | 36 | 100% | 100% |
| 2 | 1–1 or 2 | 36 | 100% | 100% |

The part of the table showing the chance to get off in one roll is most important. We don't expect you to memorize it, but we really hope that you will study it and learn how to work out these one-roll chances, for the following reasons.

First, it is crucial that you know how to move your last few men as you are bearing them off. Suppose that you have one man each on your six, five, and two points. You roll 3–2 and use the 2 to bear off your man from the two point. What do you do with the 3? If you move from the five to the two point, you leave yourself with men on the six and two points and a 36 per cent chance to get off on your next roll. If you move from the six to the three point, you leave yourself with men on the five and three points and a thirty-nine per cent chance to get off on your next roll. Clearly, this second way is correct.

Secondly, in a gambling game and in tournament play you must know when to double in situations where your opponent is sure to get off if he gets to play again (i.e., to win, you must get off in your next roll), and when to accept a double by your opponent.

As you can see in the table, when the total count for your two men is eight or more your chance to get off in one roll is always less than even money, and you should never double. When your count is seven, if your men are on the five and two points you can double; otherwise your chance is still less than even money and you should not double. In all cases where your total two-man count is six or less, you have a good double, except when you have two men on the three point.

Looking at the table with your opponent's prospects in mind, you can see that when he is down to one man on his six point he has exactly a 75 per cent chance to win, and you accept or refuse a double as you choose. At three-to-one odds, you stand to lose just as much, whether you accept or refuse.

When his two-man total is 5 or less, his chance to get off in one roll is better than 75 per cent, except in two cases. When his men are on the three and two points the chance is only 69 per cent; when they are both on the two point, the chance is only 72 per cent. You won't get rich taking doubles in those two situations, but you will lose a trifle less in the long run.

As we said, you don't need to memorize this table, but you can and should learn how to count the number of winning and losing rolls in these situations. Suppose, as an example, that your last two men are on your five and two points.

You'll get both your men off if you roll any 6 or 5 except 6–1 or 5–1. There are twenty ways of rolling a 5 or 6, and since four of them (6–1 and 5–1) don't get you off, you start with sixteen winning rolls; in addition, double 4, double 3, and double 2 will win for you, so you thus have a total of nineteen winning rolls.

Now let's check our accuracy by counting your losing rolls. You lose with any ace or with 4–3, 4–2, or 3–2. There are eleven ace rolls, and the others add up to six more, for a total of seventeen losing rolls. Thirty-six less seventeen equals nineteen winners.

The practical value of the last column of Table 4 is that it points out that you are a tremendous favorite to get off in two rolls any time that you are down to just two men in your home board. You should always double if your opponent has three or more men left to bear off, and he should refuse in all cases except one.

That one case is when both your men are on the six point, and your opponent will be able to bear off all three of his men in one roll if he gets any of the five largest doublets. If you wonder why he should accept a double when your chance appears to be 78 per cent (better than three to one), the reason lies in the fact that you may not get that second roll at all. Combining these factors leaves your net chance of winning less than 75 per cent; therefore, accepting your double is a proper gamble by your opponent, since the odds against him are less than three to one.

# 5

# GENERAL PRINCIPLES OF PLAY

Backgammon is not played in a vacuum. You have an opponent, and your plan of campaign must be to improve your position at the expense of his. It is interesting to note, and always worth bearing in mind, that backgammon is one of the few games involving both luck and skill that allows each player to see what his opponent is doing.

You must take chances. No one can win backgammon games by playing safe all the time. As a simple example, let us refer back to the opening roll of 5–2. As you saw, it isn't much of a roll but there *is* a correct way to play it. You move two men from your opponent's twelve point. One goes to safety at your eight point; the other becomes a blot on your eleven point. How does your position stand now?

First, only a 6–4 can hit that blot, a slim probability. And you lose very little even if the blot *is* hit. Your man is sent home to the bar, but you will have no trouble bringing him back into play since your opponent holds only one point in his inner board. You will have dropped behind in a running game (which will be discussed later in this chapter), but you will have three men back in his inner board, so it will be a long time before your opponent can get into a straight running game.

Now let's see what you gain by this play if you are *not* hit. Your man on the eleven point is bearing directly on your five, bar, nine, and ten points. All sorts of rolls that would have done nothing for you now become valuable. Some even become outstanding, such as 6–3 or 4–1. With 6–3 you make your five point (moving a man each from your eleven and eight points); and 4–1 enables you to make your bar point. Several other rolls are almost as advantageous.

Suppose that you play absolutely safe with your 5–2 by moving one man all the way from the enemy twelve point to your six point. Nothing can hurt you, but you haven't improved your position at all.

Of course you shouldn't take chances for the sheer joy of taking chances. Don't expose a blot to a single-number shot (a direct hit) if you have some other convenient play, unless you have something really worthwhile to gain by this exposure.

When it comes to exposing a blot you must always consider what can happen if your blot is hit. The more points your opponent has made in his inner board, the more dangerous it is to be hit (as you know from the discussion in the previous chapter). If he has made only one point in his inner board, you have thirty-five out of thirty-six chances (thirty-five-to-one odds) of coming in. If he has made two points, you have thirty-two out of thirty-six chances (eight-to-one odds); with three points made you have twenty-seven out of thirty-six chances; with four points made you have twenty out of thirty-six; and with five points made you have only eleven out of thirty-six chances of entering. If he hits you when he has a closed board (a prime of all six points in his inner board), you can't play at all until he vacates or leaves a blot on at least one point.

When you have two men on the bar and he has as many as three points made in his inner board, you have twenty-seven ways of bringing one man in on your next move, but only nine ways to bring in both. When he has four points made, leaving only two open, you have only four ways to get both men in on your next move.

Even with five points open there are eleven ways that won't bring in both men. So you always try to avoid getting two men hit at the same time. And the more points your opponent has made on his inner board, the more you try to avoid having two men off the board at all.

Conversely, you should always consider hitting two of your opponent's men if you get a chance to do so.

# Early Development

Your first aim in early play is to make your five point. This point helps to block any men your opponent has in your inner board. It puts pressure on him to avoid letting you send any of his men back home; it serves as a base of operations to bring more men into your inner board safely, and also to work on making the other points there. It will remain a tower of strength until such time as you get into a running game.

The bar point and four point are almost as valuable. The bar point gives you three good blocking points in a row (the six, bar, and eight points), but it does not give you an extra point in your inner board; while the four point still allows your opponent to play to your five point and thus get a man past two of your men.

The three point is both an asset and a liability. It does start to block your opponent's back men (and his men on the bar), but it is comparatively easy to pass, and if you then put extra men on that three point, they are practically out of play. Still, we recommend making your three point with an opening roll of 5–3. Having made the three point will become of real value if you can make the four or five point later on; and you should put even more emphasis on making those two points after you have made the three point.

As an example of this, look at Diagram 29. You opened with 5–3 and made your three point. Black rolled 4–3 and decided to move one back man to your five point and one man from your twelve point around the corner to his nine point. Now you happen to roll another 5–3.

The 5 is easy to play: move from the black twelve point to your eight point. But there are three ways to handle the 3. You can move a back man to the black four point, but this is a very poor move since any combination of 6–4, 6–2, 4–2, 4–4, or 2–2 would allow him to "point" on you there. You can move from your six point to your three point; this leaves you completely safe but in a poor position since you have advanced a third man to the three point long before there is any good reason to do so.

The best play with the 3 is to hit the blot on your five

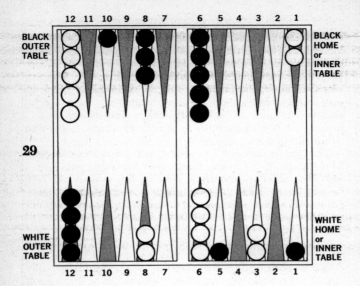

point. This play would never have been considered in the early days of modern backgammon. You are exposing a man in your home board to eighteen rolls (the man on the bar can hit you coming in with any roll containing 5, plus 4–1 and 3–2; and he can bring his man in off the bar and then hit you with his man on your one point if he rolls 4–2 or double 4). It is thus even money—eighteen out of thirty-six chances—that you will be hit; and if you are hit, a man goes all the way back from your own five point to the bar.

The modern expert doesn't care at all. He doesn't see great loss if he is hit. All it does is to give him three back men instead of two. He will plan to deploy these back men in the black inner board. If possible, he will keep one on the one point and pair the other two on the four or five point. (In any case he will maintain *some* point in the black inner board and will not split his men onto three separate points. That sort of play leads to destruction:

74

black will try to point on one of those three blots, or if black fails to point directly on you, there are any number of combination shots that will enable him to hit two of your men—even though he may leave a blot himself— and leave you with two men on the bar.)

Now look at the good side of the coin. It is also even money that he *won't* hit your blot on the five point. If he rolls double 6, double 3, or 6–3, he won't be able to play at all and will have missed an excellent roll. If he gets any of these or a playable roll that doesn't hit your blot, it will leave you ready—and probably able—to make your five point on your next roll. You would then have three good points made in your inner board, as against his solitary six point in his home board. Remember that the three point becomes a good point once you are able to make either your five or four point.

## Splitting Your Back Men

In the early days of modern backgammon it was standard tactics to split your back men, and in general to run one forward to the enemy four or five point. This advanced man would attack your opponent's outer board and even one or two points on your outer board. It would be bad luck if he were pointed on, but otherwise he would stay there until you either ran him out or brought the other back man up to pair him safely.

Today you just can't make this sort of play with the same impunity. Modern players have learned to hit this man even if they have to leave a blot in doing so.

Of course we still make this split when there is no better play or some good extra reason to do so. But, as we have said, in general the only split of the back men we do like is to move one man from the one to the two point. You don't mind being hit or even pointed on at either the one or two point, and you get a lot of advantage from this split. To begin with, you have twice as many possibilities of hitting a man in your opponent's outer board. Also, you discourage him from dropping a blot on his five point, and you are in a position where 3–2 allows you to make his four point, 4–3 to make his five point, and 6–5 to make his bar point.

As we mentioned before, moving one back man to the three point is the *least* desirable split. For example, double 5 is usually a poor roll. But when you have blots on the black one and three points you transform your opponent's double 5 into a crusher: he points on both your blots at one time (moving two men each from his eight and six points). You then have two men on the bar, while he has three points made in his inner board. But say your opponent doesn't hit you on his roll, and you then roll 3–1 or 4–2. You can make the four or five point in his board— but you pass up the chance of making the four or five point in your own inner board, as you would much prefer. In other words, the split to the black two point makes the normally poor rolls of 3–2 and 4–3 very good ones; the split to the black three point merely gives you an alternate good play with 3–1 or 4–2.

## Hitting Two Blots

We have mentioned casually that it is always good policy to hit two blots. The following example of a double hit demonstrates how important it is to learn the laws of probability as quickly as possible; we urge you once again to familiarize yourself with the previous chapter, and to *refer to it frequently as you read this book.*

In Diagram 30 you roll 4–2. The obvious play is to make your four point (moving a man each from your eight and six points). This will give you four points made in your board and a good sound position.

But if black then rolls any 2, he will bring that man off the bar and make your two point. He can then develop his own board at his leisure while you are bringing your man around and in. He is very likely to get a shot or two at you, at a time when it will cost you the game if you are hit.

Of course, if he rolls 2–5, 2–6, 1–5, or 1–6, he will be able to come in off the bar and hit one of your blots on the bar or eight point. (He should do this with 1–5 or 1–6; it is probably better just to hold your two point if he rolls 2–5 or 2–6 and to wait for the shot or shots that may come later on.)

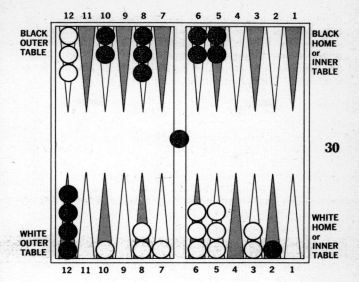

The play we recommend with 4–2 is to move a man from the black twelve to your eleven point, and to hit the blot on your two point with a man from your six point. Your opponent's best roll is then double 2, which will allow him to bring both his men in, hitting your blot on the two point, and then bringing them forward to your four point. This will actually give him a very slight over-all advantage in the game. Double 1 will allow him to bring both his men in and to your two point, hitting your blot and leaving the game almost evenly matched (you'd still have a slight advantage). With double 4 he won't hit your blot, but he will make that good advanced point in your inner board. Either 4–2 or 2–1 will allow him to bring both his men in while hitting your blot; 6–2, 5–2, and 3–2 will also enable him to hit your blot, but he'll still have one man left on the bar.

Thus, only these thirteen rolls will give him a playable game. If he rolls any one of the nine possible combinations of 6, 5, and 3, he will be left with both men on the bar and such a bad game that you will play on to try for a "gammon"; while, in a gambling game, if he rolls any of the fourteen remaining possibilities you would double him and be very pleased if he accepted the double, since a gammon is still quite possible.

## Blot-Hitting Contests

Certain games develop into blot-hitting contests. The early rolls are such that one man exposes a blot somewhere and it is promptly hit. He hits back in return, and the succeeding rolls are such that both players keep hitting and exposing men. Blot-hitting contests are apt to lead to long games, and it is good to bear in mind that there is no law compelling you to hit a blot merely because it is there. If your men are advanced a lot further than your opponent's, you don't have to worry about your chances in a running game; you do have to worry about his chances of developing a satisfactory back game against you by making and holding a couple of points in your board.

## Contact

The term "contact" is applied to all positions in which all of each player's men have not yet gotten past all of his opponent's men, and it is therefore still possible for one or both players to leave a blot or blots. When there is no more contact, you are in what is known as a "running game." In a running game the advantage lies with the player whose men are further advanced. It is important while you are still "in contact" to be able to estimate how you stand, in order to determine whether or not you should try to get past all of your opponent's men and break off contact.

There is a simple way to estimate how you stand, or "count your position," which is to count one for each of your men in your inner board; two for each man in your outer board; three for each man in your opponent's outer board; and four for each man in his inner board. If your total is smaller than his, your position is advantageous. We will amplify this discussion of how to count your position in the next chapter.

## The Running Game

At the start of the game every one of your men is in a position where you may have to expose him as a blot at some time during the game. As the game develops your men will go past your opponent's men, his will pass yours, and eventually there will be no further contact and all you will have to do will be to bring your men into your inner board and bear them off. This is known as a running game, since your object is to roll big numbers and run as fast as possible.

The advantage in a running game clearly lies with the player whose men are further advanced; even a one-point lead is worth something. *If you are ahead, you want to disengage any men that otherwise may become blots later on in order to make sure that the faster runner will win. If you are not ahead, it is better to keep contact in the hope that you will force your opponent to leave a blot for you to hit.* These two situations are illustrated in Diagrams 31 and 32.

In each instance you roll double 5. In Position 31 you are obviously ahead in the running game, so you should move the two men from black's bar point (the seven point) to your own eight point. This will make a running game of it, and you will be a long way ahead.

In Position 32 you cannot afford to move your three back men on black's bar point since you will be miles behind in the running game. Instead, you should move one back man twice, to bring him from the black bar point to your eight point; use your other two 5s to move the man from your nine point to your four point and the man on your eleven point to your six point. Black will still be far ahead, but it will not be a running game as yet since he will have to find some way to get his two men on your twelve point past the two men you've kept on his bar point. Unless he rolls a double he is going to have to leave a blot for you to aim at.

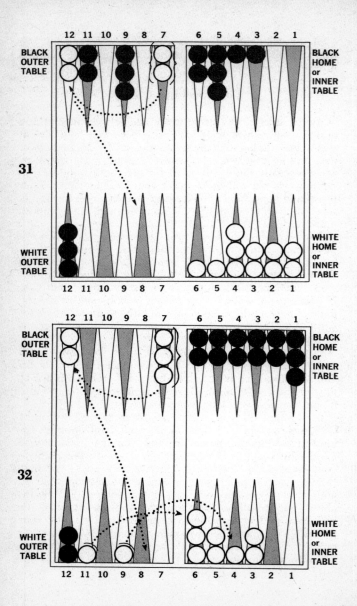

When you are in a straight running game you should try to move your men into your inner board as quickly as possible. Do not waste even an ace to move men already in the inner board. To be sure, try to distribute your men well as you move them into your inner board, rather than pile them all up on one point, but do bring them in.

## Preparing for the Running Game

To all intents and purposes, a slight interlock with your opponent still leaves a running-game position. Thus if each player's first two rolls are 6–5 and both run with their back men, all men are disengaged except that each player will have seven men left on the enemy twelve point. Theoretically, someone may have to give his opponent a shot at some point, but the chance that this will actually take place is negligible.

In slightly more complicated positions the chance is very great that a running game will develop. Even some extremely complicated positions may quickly develop into a running game, so the astute backgammon player must always consider the possibility that one will develop. If he sees that he will be ahead in a running game, he tries to simplify the position in an effort to get the running game started; if he sees that he will be behind, he tries to keep the position as complicated as possible.

In this connection, you shouldn't mind getting further behind as long as you aren't risking a gammon. In Diagram 33 you are way behind. Without bothering to count, you have three men in your opponent's inner board and only three in your own, while he has one man in your inner board and five in his own.

You roll 6–3; your best play is to hit the blot on your five point with your man on his eleven point. You don't mind if he hits you back; you hold his five point and are in no danger of being gammoned, and with four men back you can expect to get a shot at him later on after you have built up some sort of board against him. If he doesn't hit your blot on your five point, you have a good start toward making that key point and have also slowed him down a trifle.

In Diagram 34 you also roll 6–3. You can see that your

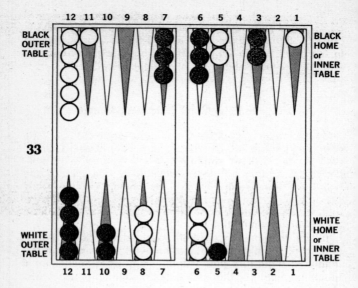

running-game position is superior, and your best play is to move your two men from black's nine point to his twelve point and your ten point. In effect, this makes the game a running one. (If you want to know exactly how far ahead you are, the "count" as explained in Chapter 6 shows that you will lead by 21 points after you play: your 102 to his 123.)

As we said at the end of Chapter 1, in the very early game the four back men—yours and his—are your chief concern. You want to extricate your two back men, and you want to block his two back men.

The position in Diagram 35 was reached the following way: you started with 6–3 and ran with a back man to the black ten point. Black rolled 2–1 and hit you with one of his men on your twelve point. You rolled 4–3, came in off the bar, and made the four point in his board. He made his five point with 5–1, and you made your five point with 3–1. Then he rolled double 6 and made both bar points. You now roll 5–3.

Your first thought is to bring one of your back men on black's four point to safety on his twelve point. Discard that thought quickly. Not only are you behind in the potential running game, but your blot on his four point becomes extremely weak. He can hit you with several shots, and he can point on your blot with several more.

The best way to play the roll is to move from his twelve to your eight point, and from your six to your

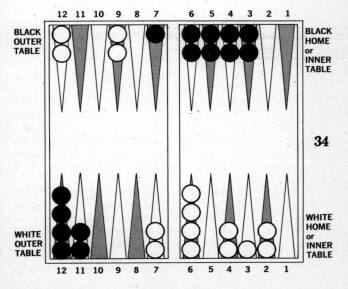

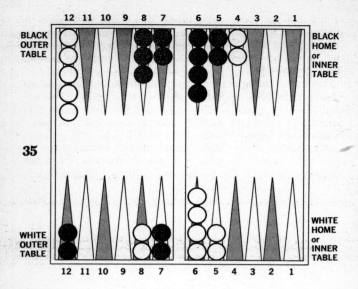

three point. You are thus getting ready to make your three point, and you plan to exert pressure on his men on your bar point. Meanwhile, your two men on his four point serve as an anchor: you are behind in a potential running game—but you aren't in a running game yet, and you aren't going to get into one if you can avoid doing so. Furthermore, you aren't in any danger of being gammoned, and your position is now only slightly worse than his.

After you play 5–3 the way we have suggested, black rolls 5–4. He is immediately embarrassed. He can play safe by moving two men from his six point, or one man from his six and another from his eight; but if black is smart, he will run his two back men on white's bar point to the white twelve and eleven points.

This produces Position 36: black has a man exposed to

any 2; and if you roll 2–3 or 2–5 you will be able to hit his blot, cover your own blot on your three point, and thus develop a good game. With any other 2 you will also hit his blot, but you won't be able to cover your blot and thus will be exposed to a lot of return shots. You can also hit with one of your back men on the black four point if you roll 6–4 or double 5. Indeed, the double 5 would probably win the game for you, since you can hit with one back man, bring the other out to the black nine point, and use your last 5 to cover the blot on your three point.

Thus you have a total of fourteen rolls out of thirty-six that hit (eleven 2s, plus 6–4 and double 5). Of these, 2–3, 2–5, and double 5 are very good, the others only fair. In addition, if you roll double 6, you could run with both back men and have a running game in which your position would now be equal to your opponent's.

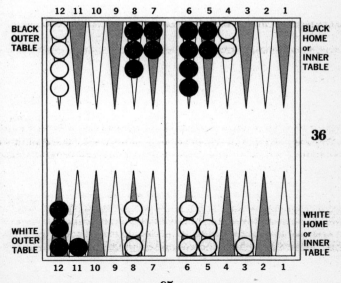

# Bearing Off

Once all men are disengaged your whole problem is to bring your men into your home board as quickly as possible and then to bear off. There isn't too much skill involved here, but in many instances there is definitely a right play and a wrong play.

As we discussed in Chapter 1, as soon as a player has brought all of his men into his inner, or home, table he can begin to take men off the board. On any given roll he may move men forward within his inner board, bear off, or both.

This brings up a very important consideration that we touched on briefly in Chapter 1: *you don't have to make the maximum move if you still play both numbers on the dice.* Now look at Diagram 37.

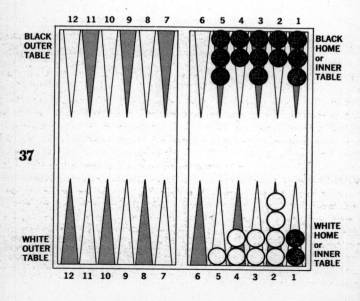

You left a blot after your last play, but your opponent failed to hit it. Now you proceed to roll either 6–1 or 5–1. You play the 1 first and use it to move your blot from the five point to the four point. Now you use the 5 or 6, as the case may be, to bear that same man off. This way you don't leave a blot. Had you played the high number first you would have been forced to use the 1 to expose a blot on your four or three point.

How should you play 6–3 in this position? You can either move forward from the five point to the two point with the 3 and then bear a man from the four point with the 6, or you can bear off the blot on the five point with the 6 and bear a man from the three point with the 3. Either play leaves a blot exposed to a direct shot.

At first glance the plays appear equal, but there is a decided advantage in making the second play: it gets two of your men off instead of only one. If black proceeds to hit your blot (wherever it is exposed), the game is likely to come down to a photo finish, and that extra man off may mean a win instead of a loss for you.

## How to Bear Off

When you are bearing off and your opponent has no men on the bar or behind you in your inner table, bear off a man in preference to moving a man within the board. The reason for this is that the more quickly you bear off your men, the fewer rolls you will need to finish the game.

When you are reduced to the last couple of men, familiarize yourself with the chances of getting them both off in one roll from various positions. You can work these out, but as a starter it would be helpful to study Table 4 on page 91 once more.

Even good players sometimes make wrong moves. Look at Diagram 38; we recently saw a good player in white's position play 6–2 badly. He wasn't very nervous about the game. He used the 6 to take his man off the six point; but he used his 2 to move from the five to the three point, instead of moving his man on the three point down to the one point.

Black rolled 5–1 and made his best play, which was to bear off the man from the five point and move a man from the four to the three point. The wisdom of this play, and the folly of white's, became apparent a moment later. White rolled 6–2 again and of course could get only one man off; black rolled double 3, bore all three of his men off, and won the game.

White was unfortunate enough to lose the game because of the way he played the 6–2, but it was a bad play, properly punished. Leaving himself with two men on his three point meant that he had only seventeen rolls (see Table 4) that would get both these men off. Those seventeen rolls were any combination of 3, 4, 5, and 6, plus double 2.

If he had used his 2 to move from the three point to the one, he would have left himself with one man each on the five and one points, and he would then have had twenty-three possible winning rolls. These rolls would have been

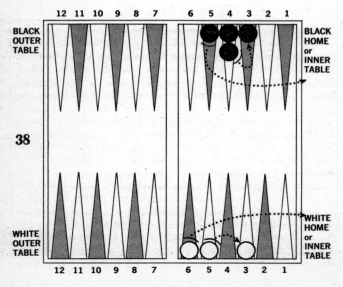

any roll with a 6 or 5, plus double 4, double 3, and double 2.

As another example, suppose that you have borne off all but two men and they are left on your four and six points. You roll 3–2. Apart from the fact that you aren't happy with that roll, you have two ways to play it. You can play it so you'll be left with men on the four and one points, or on the three and two points.

If you leave them on the four and one points, you will be able to win the game at your next throw unless you roll 3–2, 3–1, 2–1, or double 1. In other words, you have seven bad rolls and twenty-nine good ones.

On the other hand, if you leave them on the three and two points, you won't get off with any roll that includes a 1. There are eleven of these bad rolls as against twenty-five good ones—so you clearly want to move your men to the four and one points.

Eventually you should learn how to compute your chance of getting off in one roll. For practice, why not take pencil and paper right now and figure out a few other positions? If you want to check your computations, you can do so by referring to Table 4.

# 6

# COUNTING THE POSITION

Under "Contact" in the previous chapter we gave you a quick method to judge your relative standing in a running game. Such approximate ways of counting your position will do if you just want to be a pretty good player— but if you want to be a really great backgammon player, you must learn how to make accurate counts.

The count represents the total number of points you would have to move to bear off all your men *assuming no waste motion.* This is of course hypothetical, since there is always going to be wasted motion due to the fact that you tend to bear off men from the higher-numbered points first, and invariably come down to a position in which first your six point, then your five point, and then the four and three points have no men left on them, so that you don't get full value out of any numbers on the dice except 1 and 2.

However, it stands to reason that in most running-game positions you can measure your relative standing by this optimum count.

The count of each man in your own board is that of the point he is on. Thus, a man on your six point is counted at 6, while three men on that point would be counted at 18; a man on your bar point is counted at 7, and so on. The count for men in your opponent's board starts with 13 for each man on his twelve point (since he is 13 moves away from bearing him off), 14 for men on his eleven point, and so on up to 24 for each of your men on his one point. One way to determine the exact count for these men is to count the number of pips (points) necessary to bring them to the black twelve point and then to add 13 for each such man.

Thus, in Diagram 39 your count is 109. This is made up of 30 (the two men on the black ten point); 26 (the two men on the black twelve point); 9 (the man on your nine point); 18 (the three men on your six point); 15 (the three men on your five point); 4 (the man on your four point); 3 (the man on your three point); and 4 for the two men on your two point.

The black count is 118, represented by 52 for his four men on your twelve point; 18 for the two men on his nine point, and 8, 7, 12, 10, 8, and 3 for the rest of his men.

Notice that this isn't entirely a running-game position yet. There is still contact between your men in black's outer board and his men in yours; there is some slight chance that one of you will have to leave a shot, but this chance is small enough to be ignored. Thus, this may be considered a straight running-game position.

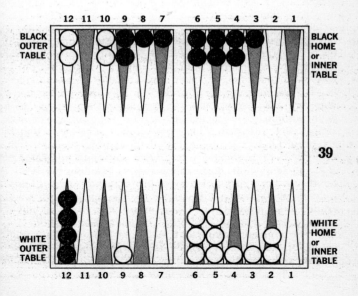

There is an alternate and quicker way to count the position: you work on differences. Your four men on the black ten and twelve points are a total of 4 points worse than your opponent's four men on your twelve point. You begin by counting 4 against yourself. Your man on the nine point cancels out one of his two men on his nine point. This leaves him with one other man on the nine point and single men on the eight and seven points. The three count 24 (9+8+7) against him, and after taking out the 4 you were behind, you come into the home boards with a 20-point advantage.

You lose 11 of this 20 here. The extra man on your six point counts 6 against you; the extra man on your five point counts 5 against you; your man on the four point balances one of his two men on the four point so you gain 4 here for a net so far of 7 behind in the home boards; the single men on the three points cancel each other out, while the two men on your two point cost you 4 more to bring the home board net to minus 11. Subtracting that from the 20 you were ahead outside the home boards leaves your final position 9 points better than (i.e., less than) your opponent's.

In using the count to decide whether or not to double, bear in mind that the average roll in backgammon has been computed to be 8⅙, allowing for the extra plays with doubles; so if it is your roll, you have a decided advantage in this case: 9 points plus whatever your roll will be. If it is your opponent's roll, you still have an advantage, but it is a very small one. Assuming it is your roll, is your position good enough to double? The answer is— almost! But with such a long way to go it is better to wait a few rolls before losing control of the doubling cube.

While the exact count is important, you must add some common sense to it. Some running-game positions are better than others. It is a matter of just where your men are located. In general, it is better to have men scattered around than grouped on a few points. For example, you almost never get full advantage of your rolls if all your men are grouped on your one, two, and three points. The count for those men is small indeed, but the count is misleading since (unless you roll a double) you can't bear off more than two men in any one roll. As an extreme example, suppose that you have borne off ten men and have five left on your one point. Your count is 5, but barring doubles you need three rolls to get off. Even with a double, you still need two rolls.

But let's say that your opponent has borne off thirteen men and has two men left on his six point. His count is 12, but he can get off in *one* roll with double 6, double 5, double 4, or double 3, and his chance of getting off in two rolls (see Table 4) is 78 per cent. In terms of odds, his chance of getting off in one roll is one in nine (the above four rolls out of thirty-six); the odds in favor of his getting off in two rolls are one hundred sixty-nine to forty-seven, or slightly better than three and a half to one. Thus, even though your count is only 5, with your five men on the one point you are a decided underdog.

Suppose that you have two men left on the six point and he has three men on his one point. It is your roll. Should you double? This question will be answered in the next chapter!

## Counting the Number of Turns Left

At a certain stage of the running game you should forget about points and just count the number of rolls each of you should need to end the game.

Except for the position in which all your men are on your one and two points with at least half of them on the one point, there is always a chance that repeated bad rolls will cause you to miss, but if your men are all well forward in your board, you should just treat this as an unacknowledged possibility and not really allow for it.

Take this example: you have two men each on your one, two, and three points. You expect to get off in three rolls, but there is a 2½ per cent chance that you will need four. Don't worry about this; estimate three rolls.

Suppose that you are down to twelve men, placed two each on your one to six points. Should you expect to get off in six rolls? Decidedly not. The odds are that you will miss at least once. Can you afford to estimate seven rolls here? Yes, you can! You can miss twice and still get off in seven rolls. The first miss will leave you with an odd number of men and cost you a roll, but the second miss will cost you nothing. It will merely give you an even number again.

This is most important: when you have an odd number of men, you can afford to miss bearing off two men on one roll without costing yourself a turn; when you have an even number of men, just one miss will cost you a full roll. It may seem obvious, but think about it and remember it!

## Doubling and Redoubling after Counting the Number of Turns Left

When it is your roll and both you and your opponent need the same number of rolls to get off, you have an obvious advantage. In any such position, if the doubling cube is still in the middle, you should make the first double—provided that your chance to get off on schedule is at least slightly better than your opponent's.

Suppose that you and your opponent each have fourteen men placed forward in your inner boards. It is a seven-roll situation for each of you. If your men are placed just the least bit farther forward than his, you should double. If they are placed the same or worse, don't double. Wait a roll or two!

Furthermore, don't be as quick to redouble as you may be to offer the first double. Remember that a redouble moves the doubling cube from your side of the table to his. This consideration is important enough so that you definitely should *not* redouble when there is a six-turn-against-six-turn position (that is, twelve men against twelve men) or a five-turn position (ten men against ten men) in which your opponent has all of his men down on his one and two points.

In a four-turn position (eight men against eight men) you have a good situation in which to redouble. He should accept if all his men are on his one and two points, but he should refuse if two of his men are on his three point (or higher, of course). The reason for this is that he won't bear off four men with double 1 or double 2, so that those two doubles won't save him a roll.

In a three-turn position, he should refuse your double.

To win he needs to roll a doublet on one of two turns, and even if he rolls one at his first turn, he gets no chance to redouble you since you will either win or lose the game on your second roll.

Now that we've given you a taste of doubling strategy, it's time to explore fully this fascinating part of the game.

# 7

# DOUBLES AND REDOUBLES

The doubling cube is used to double the stakes for which you are playing.

We don't know who first added the doubling feature to backgammon, but we feel we owe him a great debt. Without the doubling feature, few people would be playing backgammon today, and we probably wouldn't have written this book.

It is difficult to imagine anyone reading this book who will never play backgammon for money, or play in a tournament, but we urge even that rare enthusiast to read this chapter carefully. An understanding of the thinking behind doubling strategies will help anyone to play backgammon more skillfully.

We warn you that some of our discussion will be very tough going, but don't get discouraged! Whatever you may not fully comprehend the first time will be clearer after reading later chapters. But now is the time to start.

Before the game begins the doubling cube is placed in the middle of the board on the bar, with the number 64 on top and facing left or right (i.e., not facing either player directly). This of course does not mean that you're playing for sixty-four units; rather, it reminds both players that you are starting at one unit.

If there is an automatic double, the number 2 is faced, again left or right; if there is a second automatic double, the number 4 is faced, and so on. The cube is left in the same position until the first double during play, to indicate that either player has the right to double when it is his turn to play.

# Automatic Doubles

These have no official part in backgammon: they are not allowed in tournaments, and in most expert games they are either barred completely or else limited to one. But if both players agree, an automatic double occurs at the beginning of a game if both players, in tossing for first play, roll the same number. They may repeat tossing the same number several times, so even in a small-stake game it is best to limit automatic doubles to one, or perhaps two. Remember that three automatic doubles multiply the original stake by eight, not three!

Some people like to liven up the game by simply starting the cube at 2—and after a few drinks possibly starting at 4 or even 8. This can be a dangerous procedure and can change a friendly game for small stakes into a heavy gambling game that can get quite out of hand.

You won't get into this kind of trouble if you restrict yourself to one or two automatic doubles. Be very wary of anyone who suggests unlimited automatic doubles.

# Regular Doubles

After the first roll either player may double at any time when it is his turn to roll. He should consider doubling when he gains an advantage, small or large, during the course of the game.

Normally, if he decides to double, he picks up the doubling cube, turns it to the 2 (or, if it's a redouble, the next higher number—4, 8, 16, etc.) and places it near his opponent's side of the table, usually saying, "I double."

His opponent must then decide whether the doubler's position is too advantageous to allow him to risk accepting the double. If he decides to refuse the double, the game is then over and the doubler wins whatever the stake was before his double.

If he decides to accept the double, he usually says "Yes" and moves the doubling cube nearer to his side of the table. The game then continues at the new stake, which is double the old. Thus, if you have been playing for a dollar a game, the stakes become two dollars a game.

After the double is accepted, the person doubling cannot make the next double, no matter how much his advantage may grow as the game progresses. The man who has been doubled is then the only one who has the right to redouble, and the doubling block is now said to be "in his control." He may double any time it is his turn, before he rolls his dice, if and when he finds himself ahead in the game.

He would then say "I double," and if it is accepted he turns the cube to 4 (or whatever is then the next higher number) and moves it to his opponent's side.

Later we will analyze in detail how and when to double, but first there are some general principles worth keeping in mind:

As we have often urged, you should learn how to figure odds, both in order to know when to double and so that when you are doubled you can figure your chances of winning the game. In most situations if you are at only a slight disadvantage, you ought to accept your opponent's double. Even though the odds are slightly against you at that moment, the fact that the doubling cube then reverts to your control improves your odds. More on this later.

Before accepting any double, always make sure that you are not in danger of losing a gammon (which doubles the stake) or a backgammon (which triples it).

In deciding whether or not to accept your opponent's double, bear in mind that many average players tend to accept doubles that are too risky. Especially in the running game, the average player will rise to the bait and chance it, hoping for a lucky roll (such as double 6), which would turn the advantage to him. Remember, your opponent has just as much chance as you of rolling that double 6.

There are both tangible and intangible factors to weigh in deciding whether to double, and whether to accept your opponent's double. These include how good a player your opponent is; whether he usually accepts or turns down close doubles; how erratic a player he is; and how high the stakes are already.

The better the game, the fewer doubles and redoubles.

If you see a game with the cube bouncing back and forth like a ping-pong ball, you'll be watching an exciting game—but you won't be watching good backgammon.

A player who knows when to double and when not to double is probably an expert. If he also knows when to *refuse* a double, there is no question about it: he *is* an expert.

The point is not that doubles aren't made and accepted in expert games, but rather that doubles don't come so frequently that the stakes end up at 32, 64, or higher. Quite the contrary: few games between experts go beyond 4, and a 16 game is almost as rare as a baseball no-hitter.

An early book on backgammon contained the absurd statement: "In a perfect game no double will ever be accepted."

You might be inclined to doubt that such a statement is absurd, arguing as follows: clearly, no expert would ever offer to double unless the odds were in favor of his winning, and equally clearly, no expert would ever accept a double under conditions which favored his opponent.

The real point at issue, however, is: how much do the odds favor the doubler? Let's consider a simple situation. It's my roll. I have two men left on the board; one is on the two point and one is on the four point. My opponent has one man left on the one point. Thus, unless I win on this roll, he is certain to win on his next. A quick count will show that of the thirty-six possible outcomes of my next roll, I will win the game if I get one of the twenty-three rolls that are favorable to me and I will lose it if I get one of the thirteen unfavorable rolls (any 1 and 2–3). If I roll without offering to double I have a probability of 23/36 of winning the game at the present stakes (which we'll call one unit) and 13/36 of losing that one unit, giving me a *net* "positive (or plus) expectation" of 23/36 less 13/36 or 10/36 of one unit. If I double and the double is accepted, my "plus expectation" also doubles and becomes 10/36 of *two* units, or, what is the same thing here, 20/36 of one unit. Hence, I double. You may still say that no expert would accept such a double since it is so crystal clear that the double is to my advantage. So let us examine the situation from my opponent's point of view.

If he accepts the double, he has a net "negative expectation" of 20/36 of one unit (simply, the reverse of my plus expectation); but if he refuses the double, he has a *certainty of minus one whole unit*. He would be very foolish to refuse to accept the double—he would have preferred that I hadn't doubled but, once I did, he had no intelligent alternative but to accept!

It was fairly easy to work out your plus expectation in the preceding situation. You were either going to win or lose the game depending on your next roll, and since you were more likely to win the game than to lose it, you had a good double. Specifically, your plus expectation if you failed to double was 10/36. The double increased this to 20/36 and hence the right to double in this position was worth 10/36 of a unit.

It was also correct for your opponent to accept. Refusal would have cost him one unit; acceptance gave him a "minus expectation" of 20/36 of that unit, so that his right to accept your double was worth 16/36 or 4/9 of that unit.

Just what is meant by a "plus expectation"? All this means is that the odds are in your favor, and the better the odds in your favor, the higher your plus expectation.

Suppose we translate your plus expectation in the previous example into money—American money, for the sake of convenience. The stake is a dollar a point; if you arrived at this particular position exactly thirty-six times, you would expect to win twenty-three dollars and lose thirteen dollars, for a net profit of ten dollars in thirty-six games, or *an average profit per game of 10/36 dollars or just under twenty-eight cents.*

By doubling the stakes you double your plus expectation to 20/36 dollars, or almost fifty-six cents.

Thus, your position is "worth" fifty-six cents to you if you double. It represents an *expected loss* or *minus expectation* of fifty-six cents to your opponent, once he accepts your double. If he refuses your double he is all through with "expectation." He can't possibly lose two dollars; but he has certainly lost one dollar, which is considerably more than the expected fifty-six-cent loss for taking the double.

It should therefore be easy to see that *in all one-roll situations you should double any time that the odds are in your favor* (i.e., when you have a plus expectation).

Suppose that your two men in the previous example were on the five and two points. You would have nineteen winning and seventeen losing rolls and thus a plus expectation of just 2/36 of a unit, or just over five cents (translating it into money at a dollar a point). A double would increase your plus expectation to eleven cents).

It should be even clearer that your opponent should accept this double. Why should he pay out a dollar for sure instead of his "expected" eleven cents?

When is a double so overwhelming that it should not be taken? The answer to this is that three-to-one odds represent the breaking point. When the odds are less than three to one in your favor, your opponent does better *in the long run* if he accepts your double. He doesn't win, but he loses less, on the average.

When the odds are more than three to one in your favor, he should refuse. His right to accept in such situations represents a liability, not an asset.

To see why this is so, let's go back to our dollar game. If the odds are three to one in your favor, your plus expectation is seventy-five cents minus twenty-five cents, or half a dollar. If you double the stakes, you double your plus expectation (and your opponent's minus expectation) to one dollar, which represents the *exact cost to your opponent if he refuses the double*.

## When to Make the First Double

Is it possible for you to have a position that is too good to double? Of course! Your opponent always has the right to refuse when you double. If you have a good chance to win a gammon, you may prefer to play on for it.

Position 40 was reached after three rolls by each player. You started with 6–5 and ran one back man to the black twelve point. Black rolled 6–4 and brought a back man to your eleven point. You rolled double 2 and made your eleven and four points, hitting his blot on your eleven point in the process. He rolled 4–1 and decided to bring

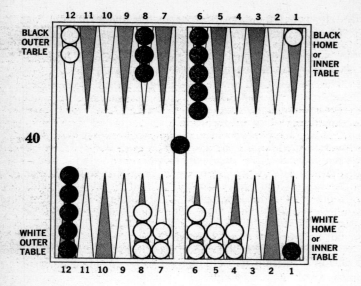

his man on the bar up to your five point. We don't approve of that play, and you might have doubled right then, but you rolled once more and got double 6. This enabled you to make your bar and five points and to put one black man back on the bar. Black proceeded to roll 6–5 and could not come in from the bar.

If you double, you will win a point, unless you are playing against someone who takes almost any double offered him. If you play on, your plus expectation is greater than that: your one-point profit is in no danger, since you can double the stake at any subsequent turn to play, and if you get a few more good rolls, you will win two points with a gammon.

For instance, suppose that black's next roll is 3–2. He comes in from the bar with the 3 and makes your three point by moving from your one point with the 2. Your chance to gammon has gone down to practically nothing, but your advantage is still overwhelming; you should now double him.

Let's consider another situation. Assume that your position is such that you estimate that you have one chance in three of winning a gammon, one chance in three of winning an ordinary game, and one in three of losing. It is your roll.

Should you double? Should your opponent accept?

If you don't double and play on, your plus expectation is two-thirds of a unit. The unit you win when you win a single game cancels the unit you lose when you lose a single game, so the two units you win for gammon produce your net plus expectation.

If you double and your double is accepted, your plus expectation doubles also and thus grows from two-thirds of a unit to one and one-third units, while if your double is refused you win one unit.

Hence you should double, and your opponent should refuse.

## A Paradox

Look at Position 41. It is your roll, and there are nineteen out of thirty-six rolls that will end the game immediately (double 6, double 5, double 4, double 3, double 2, 6–5, 6–4, 6–3, 6–2, 5–4, 5–3, 5–2). If black's two men were on his one point, you should double or redouble, and thereby double your plus expectation. But here is black with a *poorer* position than that, and this time you should not double if the cube is on your side. The reason is that if you keep the cube on your side and fail to get both your men off, *you may get a second turn*. Black has seven possible rolls that won't take both his men off.

Thus if you don't double, your chance of winning is 19/36 plus the product of 17/36 (your chance of not getting off in one roll) times 7/36 (black's chance of not getting off). This represents a total chance of winning of 803/1296 (19/36, or 684/1296, plus 17/36 times 7/36, or 119/1296); your chance of not winning is 1296 less 803, or 493 out of 1296. Thus your net plus expectation is 803/1296 minus 493/1296, which is 310/1296; to express

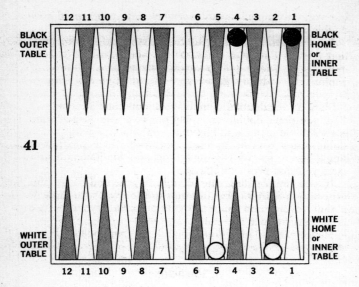

it as a decimal, divide 310 by 1296, which comes to .239 times the stake.

If you do double, your opponent will accept, and now your whole chance depends on your first roll, because if you don't get off you are going to be redoubled, and you will have to refuse. Your net plus expectation if you double is therefore 2/36 (19/36 less 17/36) times 2 (the doubled stake), which is 4/36 or .111 times the undoubled stake.

In other words, you do better than twice as well if you leave the cube alone.

## The Position of the Cube

The preceding paradox illustrates a point that is generally overlooked: it is a two fold advantage to have the doubling cube on your side of the table. The first advantage is that you can double and force your opponent to give up or to play at a doubled stake any time that it is your turn to roll. The second is that, no matter how good his position becomes, you are going to get to play the game to the finish since he can't double you.

## When to Double, Redouble, Refuse, and Accept

So far, this has been a tough chapter. We have shown a position so good that you don't want to double. We have discussed the advantage that you gain by having the doubling cube on your side of the table. We have pointed out that in the end game you should accept a double any time the odds against you are less than three to one. We have given an example of a proper double when your chance of winning is just better than even money (nineteen out of thirty-six)—and in general we've kept things at a level that has probably confused you.

*If it hasn't, you're a genius!*

Now let's see if we can't give you a few rules of thumb. We'll start by considering only cases in which there is no possibility of a gammon.

In such situations you should *consider a first double* (moving the cube from the center to your opponent's side of the bar) at any time that you estimate that the odds in your favor are seven to five, or better. You should *definitely* make a first double any time you think the odds in your favor are nine to five or better.

When there has already been at least one double, you should be a trifle more conservative about redoubling. You should *consider* a redouble when the odds in your favor are three to two, and you should *definitely* redouble when the odds are two to one in your favor or better.

Of course these doubles will all be accepted, or should be accepted. But there is no guarantee—we have seen incredible refusals and acceptances!

When you have a chance to win a gammon, you double a trifle quicker and your opponent is more likely to refuse.

So much for rules of thumb. How do you figure out what your chances are? This comes only with experience. You start by counting the position (see the previous chapter). Once you have done that, Table 5 gives a rough estimate of your chances, but *only if all else is even.*

## TABLE 5
### THE APPROXIMATE ODDS IN YOUR FAVOR WHEN IT IS YOUR ROLL IN A RUNNING GAME AND THERE IS LITTLE OR NO POSITIONAL ADVANTAGE

| Your count | Your lead over your opponent* | Odds in your favor |
|---|---|---|
| 60 | 0 | 6 to 5 |
|  | 4 | 8 to 5 |
|  | 8 | 11 to 5 |
|  | 12 | 17 to 5 |
|  | 16 | 5 to 1 |
|  | 20 | 8 to 1 |
| 70 | 0 | 11 to 10 |
|  | 4 | 7 to 5 |
|  | 8 | 2 to 1 |
|  | 12 | 3 to 1 |
|  | 16 | 4 to 1 |
|  | 20 | 6 to 1 |
| 80 | 0 | 21 to 20 |
|  | 4 | 13 to 10 |
|  | 8 | 9 to 5 |
|  | 12 | 13 to 5 |
|  | 16 | 18 to 5 |
|  | 20 | 5 to 1 |
| 90 | 0 | 31 to 30 |
|  | 4 | 12 to 10 |
|  | 8 | 8 to 5 |
|  | 12 | 12 to 5 |
|  | 16 | 16 to 5 |
|  | 20 | 9 to 2 |
| 100 | 0 | 41 to 40 |
|  | 4 | 11.5 to 10 |
|  | 8 | 3 to 2 |
|  | 12 | 11 to 5 |
|  | 16 | 3 to 1 |
|  | 20 | 4 to 1 |

* The number of *additional* points in your opponent's count.

| 0 | 51 to 50 |
| 4 | 11 to 10 |
| 8 | 7 to 5 |
| 12 | 2 to 1 |
| 16 | 14 to 5 |
| 20 | 19 to 5 |

We make no claim that this table is completely accurate, but it does represent the best experience of over thirty years of backgammon.

It should be used carefully. Thus, if you have six men on your five point and your opponent has two men each on his six, five, and four points, the count of each side is 30—*but his position is decidedly better.*

Table 6 is based upon Table 5; it presents the same information in a more usable form.

### TABLE 6
### SHOULD YOU DOUBLE?

| Your lead | Your count lies between these limits | Should you double? | Should you redouble? | Should your opponent accept? |
|---|---|---|---|---|
| 0 | 55–115 | no | no | —— |
| 4 | 55–75 | yes | no | yes |
| | 75–115 | no | no | —— |
| 8 | 55–75 | yes | yes | yes |
| | 75–115 | yes | no | yes |
| 12 | 55–75 | yes | yes | no |
| | 75–115 | yes | yes | yes |
| 16 | 55–105 | yes | yes | no |
| | 105–115 | yes | yes | yes |

Let's go back to Diagram 39 in the last chapter. Your count is 109 and your opponent's 118. The odds in your favor are better than seven to five and worse than two to one. You should double, but if you already have been doubled you should not redouble.

Table 5 shows that the odds in your favor are between seven to five and two to one: your count of 109 is closest to the 110 in the first column; your lead of 9 lies between 8 (which has odds of seven to five) and 12 (which has

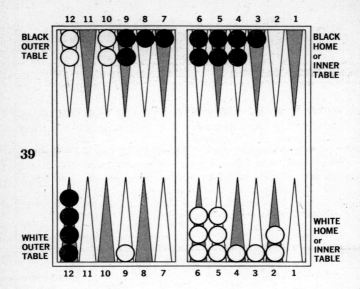

odds of two to one). Table 6 shows that you should double if the game has not yet been doubled, but you should not redouble: your lead is nearest the 8 group in the table, and your count lies between 75 and 115.

If you don't want to learn these tables (and we see no reason for you to do so unless you want to spend a large part of your life learning backgammon), here is a simple rule for doubling in a running game:

1. Count your position and your lead.

2. If your lead is as much as 7½ per cent of your count, make a first double.

3. If it is as much as 10 per cent of your count, make a first double or redouble.

4. If your opponent doubles in a running game, accept any time you are less than 15 per cent of your opponent's count behind (i.e., his lead is less than 15 per cent).

Thus, in Diagram 39 your count is 109 and your lead

over your opponent's count (118) is 9; 9 is about 8¼ per cent of your count, so you should make a first double, but you should not make a redouble.

In the last chapter we raised the question of what action, if any, you should take with the doubling cube when you have two men on your six point while your opponent has three men on his one point.

Let's begin by calculating your chance to win if the game is played to the end. You will win if you get off in one roll, or if you get a second roll and get off then.

Table 4 shows that your total chance of getting off in two rolls is 78 per cent, and of getting off in one roll 11 per cent. Hence, your chance of getting off on your second roll is the difference, or 67 per cent. However, you may not get a second roll. Your opponent has one chance in six (six possible rolls out of thirty-six) of rolling a double and winning before you get that second roll. Therefore, your chance to win is 11 per cent plus 5/6 of 67 per cent. This adds up to 67 per cent.

A probability of 67 per cent is equivalent to odds of about two to one in your favor, and so you should double or redouble, as the case may be. You may wish you hadn't redoubled if you proceed to roll 2–1 and get redoubled right back, but you should not let this possibility dissuade you.

## The Psychology of the Double

The more you play backgammon the more you'll see the importance of learning your opponent's particular habits of play—especially his treatment of the doubling cube.

Is he a quick doubler? Always hesitate before taking a double from this kind of player. He always wants you to accept. Make him worry before you do accept; he may start to double even *more* prematurely. You might even refuse one unsound double in order to get him to double even more hastily in the future.

Is he a slow doubler? Such a man really hopes that you will refuse his double. If you do refuse him, do so slowly. If you accept, do so quickly and cheerfully. He will tend to be even slower with his future doubles.

Is he inclined to refuse close doubles? You can afford some unsound doubles against him; if he refuses one out of three, you will gain.

Is he inclined to take sound doubles? Be even more sound in your doubles. They will still be accepted.

Watch how the score affects his doubling and his acceptance and refusal of your doubles. Losers tend to double unsoundly and to take doubles when they should refuse; they can't get even winning 1-point games or losing any games at all.

Winners go in the other direction. They are quick to refuse doubles and slow to turn the cube themselves. They want to stay winner and don't want to let the action speed up.

Don't be discouraged if there are things you don't understand the first time you read this chapter. Go on to the next chapters, but plan to refer here again and again.

# 8

# STRATEGY IN THE EARLY GAME

Even if you haven't done so up until now—though we hope you have—it will help you a great deal with this and later chapters if you get your backgammon board and follow each point in the discussion step-by-step, making the actual moves on your board and studying each position thoroughly.

We'll begin with an early development in which you (white, as usual) obtain a quick advantage. Your first roll is 3–1, so you get off to a good start by making your five point. Black rolls 4–2 and makes his four point. You now roll 4–1.

Your first impulse is simply to reinforce your eight point by moving a man there from the black twelve point. Resist this inclination. You want to make more points, and you should use the 4 to move one of those five men from the black twelve point to your nine point. This will leave a blot, but one that is exposed only to 6–2 or 5–3 since your men on the five point protect your blot from either double 4 or double 2.

There are alternate plays with the 1. You can split your two back men, or you can move one man from your six point to your five point. Either play is a good one, but we prefer to split the two back men. This gives you a chance to make the black five point with 4–3 or the black bar point with 6–5, and doubles your shots at any blot that black may expose in his outer board.

Black also rolls 4–1. He decides not to make your play, since if he leaves a blot on his nine point you'll be able to hit it from his two point with 6–1, 5–2, or 4–3, and from his one point with 6–2, double 4, or double 2—a total of ten shots.

Instead he decides to harass you by hitting both the blots in his board with one of the men on his six point. This forces you into the position of having to bring two men back in from the bar, and exposes him to only eleven possible return shots. And in any event he doesn't mind being hit since the game has just started and three men back may well turn out to be an advantage.

The game is now in the position illustrated in Diagram 42, and it is your roll. Any simple roll means a forced play, since you have two men on the bar, and you lose your whole roll with double 6, double 4, or 6–4. But let's see how you should play the other doubles, bearing in mind that you must start by bringing in your two men:

*Double 5.* Bring your two men on the bar all the way to the black ten point.

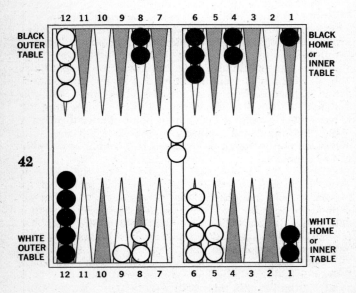

*Double 3.* Bring in your two men, then make your three point with two men from your six point.

*Double 2.* Same thing, except that you make your four point.

*Double 1.* Hit his blot and leave those two men on the black one point; then move the two men on your eight point to your bar point.

Let's say you actually roll 6–1 and use the 1 to hit the blot on the black one point. You can't bring in the other man, since the six point is held against you, so you lose that part of the roll.

Black then rolls 5–1; he brings in his man from the bar with the 1 and reinforces his eight point with the 5 (moving one of his men from your twelve point). He could have hit your blot on his one point, but he decided against that play since it would leave him with no builders at all. This way he has three men each on his six and eight points and can move one man safely from either point if the occasion arises.

His three men on your one point constitute a distinct weakness in his game, but he was forced to bring in his man on that point and couldn't move forward from it.

You now roll 5–4 and are delighted to make the black five point, coming in on the 5 and moving the 4 with the man on the black one point. Black then rolls 3–2 and uses the 3 to move a man from your one point to your four point, and uses the 2 to bring a man from his eight to his six point.

This leads to the position shown in Diagram 43. You have developed a very sound position. Your first roll enabled you to make your five point; your last roll enabled you to make the black five point. Your two men on that point allow you to take liberties with your forward men, who are placed nicely on the board.

Black, on the other hand, has a poor position. Not that he could have done much about it; he rolled poorly after his initial 4–2. If this were a gambling game, at this point you would pause to consider whether or not you should offer a double. Note that nine rolls (5–4, 5–2, 4–2, double 4, double 2, and double 1) will enable you to point on his blot so temptingly exposed on your four point (you don't, of course, consider doing so with 5–1, 4–1, or 2–1, which

113

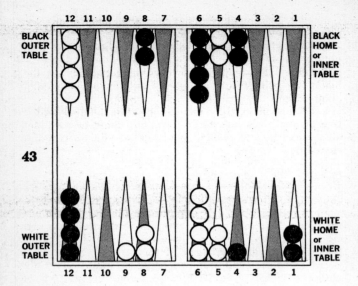

BLACK OUTER TABLE
BLACK HOME or INNER TABLE
WHITE OUTER TABLE
WHITE HOME or INNER TABLE

would necessitate leaving a blot on your most valuable five point). However, the other twenty-seven rolls wouldn't be as good, so you decide not to offer a double at this point, and just roll. Let's see exactly how you should handle various throws that you might get at this point:

*Double 6.* Make your bar point with two men from the black twelve point, and bring the men on the black five point to the black eleven point. You can't do anything about the blot on your nine point, but it will be no tragedy if black hits him.

*Double 5.* You have several choices with this roll. You can bring your two men forward from the black five point all the way to your ten point; this will bring more guns to bear on black's blot on your four point. Or you can move two men from the black twelve point to your three point. Either of these plays leaves your blot on the nine point exposed to a 5 or a 6–2. If black rolls one of those numbers, he will hit your blot; if he rolls a 3 or the right small combination, he would be wise to make your four point instead.

Both these plays with double 5 are good, but a far better play is to use two of your 5s to make your three point with the men on your eight point; use one 5 to hit his blot with the man on your nine point, and use the last 5 to move a man from the black twelve point to your eight point. This is a very aggressive play, since you will be leaving a long-range blot on your eight point in addition to the unavoidable direct blot on your four point. If your opponent rolls double 4, he will hit both of them; if he rolls any other 4, 3–1, or double 2, he will hit the blot on your four point; if he rolls 6–2, he will hit the blot on your eight point. This adds up to a total of sixteen possible good rolls for him, but not one of those sixteen will give him more than an evenly matched game with you. On the very bad side, his man will have to stay on the bar if he rolls any one of the nine combinations of 6, 5, and 3, and he will still have a poor game if he rolls any of the remaining eleven numbers that will enable him to enter from the bar without hitting you.

Two important basic principles of backgammon are illustrated here. The first is familiar to you by now: when you have to expose a blot to a direct shot (called a "direct blot"), expose it where it will do you the most good if it isn't hit. The second principle is that when you have to leave a blot exposed to a direct shot, it is nearly always advisable to hit an enemy blot rather than to leave him with full freedom to play his next roll. Remember, any time you put one of his men on the bar there is a chance that he will roll badly and be unable to play anything at all.

*Double 4.* Hit his blot on your four point with the two men on your eight point. Then, either move two men from the black twelve point to your nine point or move one man all the way to your five point. If black doesn't make an exceptionally good return roll, in a gambling game you would then be able to double the stake, and black would probably give up and start a new game.

*Double 3.* Move two men from the black twelve point to your bar point.

*Double 2.* Make your four point with two men from your six point, hitting his blot. Use the other two moves to bring up one man from the black twelve point to make your nine point.

**115**

*Double 1.* Either use all four moves to make your four point and his blot (with two men from your six point); or use two moves to hit his blot on your four point with a man from your six point and the other two moves to make your bar point with the two men on your eight point.

*6–5.* At first glance this doesn't look like much of a roll, but a further look discloses that you can move a man all the way from the black five point to join the man on your nine point.

*6–4.* One of the few bad rolls in this position. We favor the play of moving two men from the black twelve point. One secures your nine point; the other becomes a blot on your bar point. Twenty-four rolls can hit that blot (any 6 or 3, plus 5–1 and 4–2) but it is no great loss to you, and if black does not hit the blot, you'll have a sure-fire position in which to double the stakes, it is so strong. All other plays with this roll leave you with an unsound position.

*6–3.* Make your three point (move the man on your nine point and one of those on your six point).

*6–2.* Make your bar point (move a man each from the black twelve and your nine points).

*6–1.* Not much of a roll, for once. We would move the blot from your nine to your three point, and a man from your six to your five point. Alternative plays of moving a man from the black five point to the black twelve point as the complete roll, or of moving to the black eleven point with the 6 and moving the man on your nine point to safety with the 1, both weaken your game.

*5–4.* Make your four point, hitting his blot (move the man on your nine point and one of the men on your eight point).

*5–3.* Hit the man on your four point with your man on the nine point, and move a man from the black twelve point to your ten point. The reasons for making this play are essentially the same as those we gave for the double 5 play recommended earlier.

*5–2.* A very good roll. Make your four point, hitting his blot.

*5–1.* Hit the blot on your four point with your man on the nine point, and move a man from your six point to your five point. If your blot survives, you have an excellent game; if it is hit, you still have a sound position.

4–3. Make your nine point with one man from the black twelve point, and expose a blot on your ten point with another.

4–2. Make your four point (moving a man each from your eight and six points), leaving two long-range blots on your eight and nine points but hitting his blot.

4–1. Make your nine point with a man from the black twelve point, and move a man from your six to your five point.

3–2. Not too good a roll. Just hit his man on your four point with the man on your nine point.

3–1. Make your nine point with a man from the black twelve point.

2–1. Use the 2 to hit the blot on your four point, and move from the nine to eight point with the 1. Alternatively, it is just about as good a play to make your bar point and leave a blot on your eight point.

Note throughout this discussion that you should make no effort to play safe in this fine position but should endeavor to improve it still further with whatever roll you make. In a gambling game you will be trying to gain sufficient advantage to make an early double, and you will do so unless black's reply to your roll is a good one. At the same time, your position is so sound that even a perfect reply by black won't destroy your entire advantage. The men on black's five point constitute a safety anchor in case your opponent hits any blot you may leave.

Let us assume that in fact you throw the very good roll of 5–2 and make your four point, putting black's blot on the bar. He rolls 6–5 and can't move. You are now in Position 44.

In a gambling game your position is now good enough to warrant your doubling the stakes, and black would be wise to refuse and start a new game. The reason you would double him here is that you prefer a bird in the hand to two in the bush. You are giving up a possible gammon—but getting that bird in hand. Furthermore, there is always a chance that a desperate black may accept your double on the basis of the anchor he holds on your one

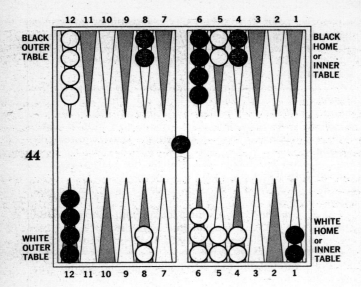

point. This anchor means that no matter how badly the next several rolls may treat him, black will still have the possibility of getting a shot at you toward the end that might win the game for him.

In our next game you start off badly. Your first roll is 6–2, and you make the aggressive move of a man from the black twelve point to your five point. Black rolls 4–3. He hits your blot on the five point with the 4 and brings a man around the corner to his ten point with the 3.

Your second roll is 5–1. You come in with the 5 and use the 1 to hit the man on your five point with one of the men on your six point. You have started to go back and don't mind the possibility of getting another man sent home. Black rolls 5–1 this time and uses the 5 to come in and hit your man on your five point. Then he uses the 1 to hit your man on *his* five point. This brings us to Position 45.

Things have started out badly, but black has not developed too good a game as yet. You have four back men (including two off the board), but he has yet to make a second point in his board.

You roll 4–2 and bring both your men in from the bar. Black rolls 4–1. He uses the 1 to make his five point and the 4 to make your five point. He could have moved the blot on his ten point to safety at his six point, but that is the sort of safety play that is penny-wise and pound-foolish. He doesn't care if that man on his ten point is hit; he will still be ahead in a potential running game, and with both five points made he has much the better of the position.

You roll 5–2. The 2 is very useful since it allows you to make the black four point using your man on the black two point. The best you can do with the 5 is to move a man from the black twelve point to your eight point. Black rolls 4–1 again and makes his nine point. We are now in Position 46.

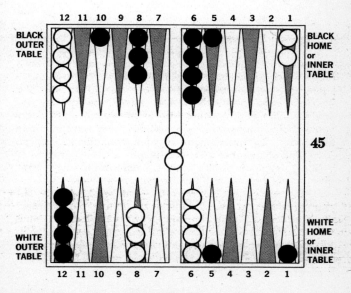

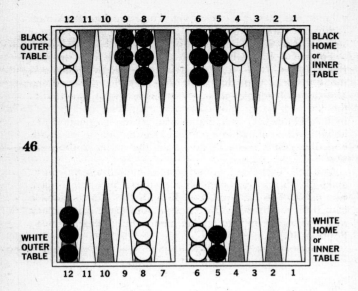

You have the poorer game at this point, but black has a lot of work to do, and your four back men are going to annoy him as he tries to capitalize on his advantage. You won't be able to hold these four men there forever, and you wouldn't mind getting still a fifth man back to delay yourself. Therefore, when you roll 6–2, you move one man from the black twelve point to your bar point and a man from your six point to your four point.

Some people in black's position would double right now. We do not recommend this. In fact, if we were white we would welcome a double: white does have slightly the poorer game, but the advantage of getting the doubling cube on our side of the board would more than compensate. We discussed this point at length in Chapter 7; for the present, just recall that when the cube is on your side of the table you are the only player with the right to turn it higher, and that this represents a decided advantage.

Here black is too smart to double. He rolls 5–4 and moves a man from your five point to his eleven point. This brings us to Position 47.

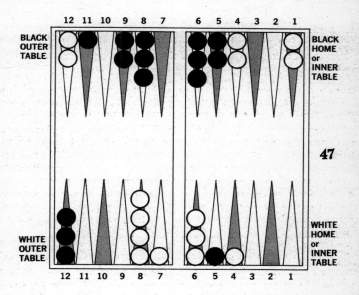

47

Black didn't have to leave a blot anywhere with his 5–4, but he wanted to get those two back men farther around before you could improve your board and while you still had a blot on it. You proceed to roll 6–3. You have a number of ways to play that roll, but none is very good. The best of a bad lot is to make your bar point with the 6, and to use the 3 to bring a man from the black one point to the black four point. Black then rolls 3–1. He could use the 1 to hit your blot on the black twelve point but sees no reason to do this. He doesn't need or want to give you a fifth man back at this point, and instead he makes his ten point, moving a man from the white twelve point and the man on his eleven point. This brings us to Position 48.

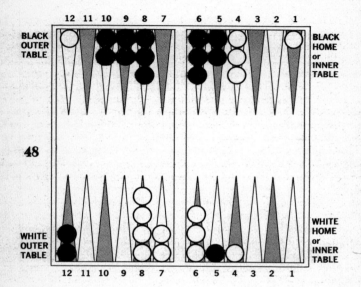

Black now has a very sound game, and your position has deteriorated. You are too far behind to compete in a running game, and you aren't far enough behind to hold a back game. You need a good roll right now.

Assume for a moment that you're in a gambling game, and let's take a careful look at the rolls that are good enough to keep black from trying to double you at this point—or good enough so that if he does double you, you can accept. They are:

*Double* 3. You use two of the 3s to hit the blot on your five point with two of the men on your eight point; then cover the blot on your four point with one of the men on your bar point, and move the man on the black twelve point to your ten point.

*Double 2.* Use two of the 2s to hit the blot on your five point with the two men on your bar point; cover the blot on your four point with a man from your six point, and move the man on the black twelve point to your eleven point.

*Double 1,* and *3–1.* Make your five point, hitting your opponent's blot (in both cases moving one man each from your eight and six points). Don't bother to protect the man on your four point. If he is hit, you have a good potential back game; if he is not hit, you have an excellent chance to make five points in a row.

*6–5* and *5–3.* Re-establish the black twelve point (with 6–5, move your man on the black one point; with 5–3, move one of the men on the black four point).

*6–3.* Make the black bar point with your man on the black one point and one of your men on the black four point.

*4–3* and *3–2.* Hit the man on your five point with the 3, and cover the blot on your four point with the 2 or 4 (as the case may be).

*4–1.* Cover the blot on your four point with the 4, and hit his blot on your five point with the 1.

If you roll any of these seventeen rolls, you will have an equal or nearly equal game in spite of your generally bad dice earlier. In a gambling game black may double, but you have good enough odds and should accept a double. With the other nineteen possible rolls, plan to give up the game if black doubles. You will never go broke refusing doubles in bad positions—and there is always another game.

# 9

## SOME LATE POSITIONS

### The Closed Board

The most comfortable late-game position is for you to have a closed board (i.e., you control all six points on your inner table) and your opponent has one or more men on the bar. If nobody has doubled or it is your turn to redouble, you should either double (and presumably end the game since your opponent will refuse the double) or play on for a possible gammon. In either instance you hope to bring the rest of your men around to your home board and then to bear them off without allowing your opponent to get a shot. You may not always be able to achieve this, even with the most careful playing. In any event your first problem is to bring your outside men past any point or points that your opponent may control outside your home board.

Note in Position 49 that if you roll either double 3 or double 4, you will be forced to break your board. With double 3 you can move two men from the black bar point to the black ten point, but you will then have to move two men in your own inner board from your six point to your three point. With double 4, your two back men will be blocked; you can move three 4s with your man on the black ten point, but you will still be forced to move one man inside your inner board. So your correct play would be to move that man on the black ten point eight spaces to your bar point, and then move two men from your six point to your two point. This way you at least avoid leaving a direct blot.

This illustrates an interesting point. Doubles are usually

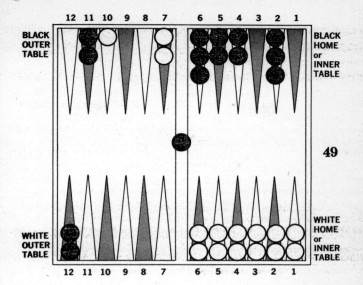

very good rolls, but you are forced to play them, and in
many positions the forced play of the wrong double will
turn out to be anything from embarrassment to total
disaster.

In this case your double forces you to break your board,
but the chances are you won't be hurt. However, suppose
that you followed that first double 3 with another double 3.
You would then be compelled to give up both your five
and four points, and the three men still stuck on the black
ten point would be orphans in the storm. You may roll a
good double and get them out of trouble, but the chances
are that you will have to give your opponent several shots
at you and lose the game.

Let's assume that your actual roll is 4–1. If you're a
careless player, you might just move the man on the black
ten point to your own ten point. This play will leave you
in trouble if your next roll is double 4.

Suppose that you guard against this by moving a man

from the black bar point to the black twelve point. This looks perfectly safe. You can then play double 4 or double 3 with ease—but suppose that your next roll is an innocuous double 1. Try to play it without breaking your board! You won't be able to, because you won't be able to play more than three of them with your outside men.

The correct way to play your 4–1 is to move the man on the black ten point to your eleven point, and one man from the black bar to the black eight point. Now you'll be able to play any subsequent roll in safety.

Even when you aren't concerned with getting past road blocks, you still want to bring in your men in such a way that you avoid leaving a blot once you are forced to break your board. There is no sure protection against the worst possible series of rolls; your plan must be to protect yourself as much as possible.

Look at Diagram 50. You are in no immediate danger since you can play any double satisfactorily. You roll 3–2—

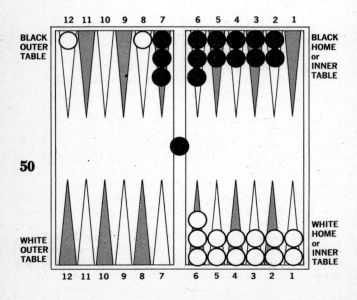

**50**

BLACK OUTER TABLE

BLACK HOME or INNER TABLE

WHITE OUTER TABLE

WHITE HOME or INNER TABLE

and right here is a good place to separate the sheep from the goats. Believe it or not, you can play this innocuous little roll very badly.

Suppose you move that man on the black eight point to your own twelve point. It looks perfectly safe and it is—for one roll. But suppose you followed this roll with double 6. Two 6s will bring the man from the black twelve point to your one point; the other two will bring the man on your twelve point to your six point and then off the board. This leaves Position 51.

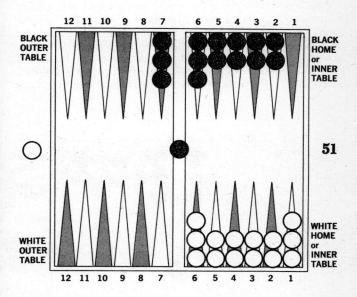

That one white man to the left of the board is the man you have just borne off. Since you have a closed board, it is your roll again immediately, and there are now lots of rolls that will force you to give your opponent an immediate shot. Specifically, if you roll double 6, double 5, 6–5, 6–4, 6–3, or 6–2, you will be forced to leave a blot, while any number of other rolls which will be temporarily safe may lead to further embarrassment.

Go back to Diagram 50 for a moment; the correct play with that 3–2 would be to move just three points with your man on the back eight point, and to move one of the men on your six point to the four point, which gives you Position 52. Look at your own backgammon board; check this position on it (we hope you've been following *all* our discussion on it) and you'll find that you can handle any combination of two rolls with complete safety.

Now let's go back to Position 50 again. This time assume that you roll 2–1. You would seem to have no worries, and without paying any attention to what may happen next, you move the man on the black twelve point to your eleven point and one man on your six point to your five point. Then you roll double 6—and you are forced to leave a blot on your six point. Could you have avoided this? Easily. In fact, you found the only way to get your-

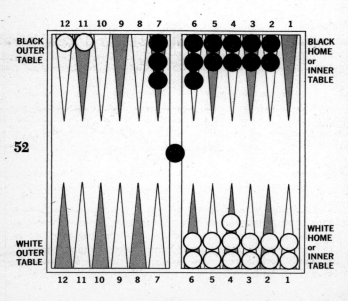

self into trouble. Any other play with that 2–1 would have left you absolutely safe.

If you play enough backgammon, this type of carelessness will prove very costly.

## Breaking Your Board

There is practically no position that is proof against perverse dice. Look at Position 53, which is considered the dream position from which to start bearing off your men. You have all of your men in your inner board, and there is no combination of two rolls that will force you to leave a blot. Now suppose that you roll 6–2: the play is just about forced. You bear a man from your six point and move a man from your five to your three point. You then roll 6–1. You bear one man from your six point and move the other to your five point. This brings you to the position shown in Diagram 54. Black now has a chance to enter and thus

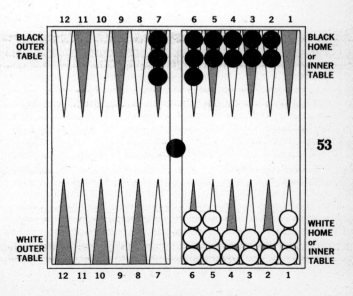

**53**

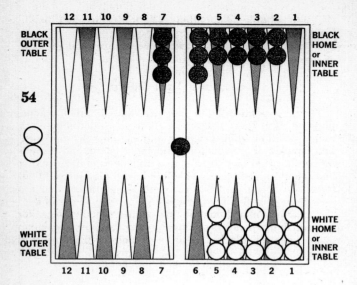

**54**

can roll again. If black rolls a 6 right away your troubles are over, but let's assume that he does not and is still on the bar. If your next roll is double 6, double 5, double 4, 6–5, 6–4, or 5–4, you have to leave a blot.

Let's look at another situation. In Position 55 you have an excellent chance to win a gammon. Black has two men on the bar and several additional men he must bring into his inner board.

You roll double 1. You can bear off four men from your one point and be almost sure of winning a gammon, unless you must later leave him a shot and then get hit. You can make a more careful play of bearing first two men from the one point and moving two men from your five to your four point. Your chance to win a gammon will still be very good, and your risk of getting into trouble will be greatly reduced. If you are accustomed to wearing both suspenders and a belt, you can play even more safely by moving two men from your five point to your three point.

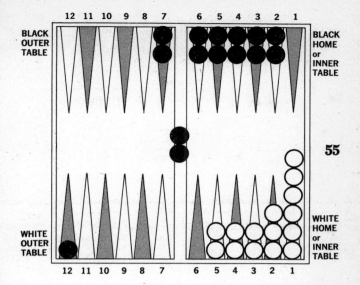

# 55

We recommend the middle course since the conservative play reduces your chance for gammon a trifle too much.

Suppose that instead of having two men on the bar, black had only one man on the bar and the other was already in his home board. Now your correct play would be to bear those four men from the one point. You need to hurry now to win that gammon, and the slight risk involved would be worth taking.

Keep in mind that when you get around to breaking your board, *the general rule is to break from the six point, then the five point, and so on.*

Thus, in Diagram 56 you have already borne off two men, and you roll 5-4. Don't bear off a man. Just move two men from your six point; you have practically no chance either to win a gammon or to lose the game—unless you leave a blot. If you use the 5-4 to bear a man off the five point and move the other man down, and

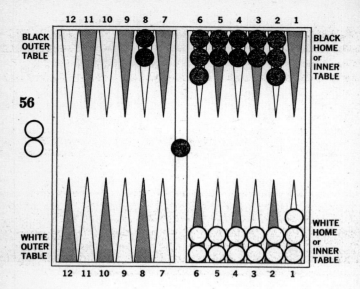

**56**

happen then to throw 6–1 or 5–1, you will be forced to leave a blot.

There is one important exception to this rule of breaking from the highest point. Suppose, in Position 56, that you roll 5–1. If you break from the six point, you'll be in Position 57. If black fails to enter and you roll double 6, double 5, double 4, 6–5, 6–4, 6–3, 6–2, 5–4, 5–3, or 5–2 (a total of seventeen rolls), you will have to leave a blot.

The correct play is to break from the five point, producing Position 58. In this position you will have to leave a blot only if you roll double 6, double 5, double 4, 6–1, or 5–1 (a total of only seven bad rolls).

### Enemy Men on Your One Point

When you have trapped two or more of your opponent's men on your one point, they are going to be there until

132

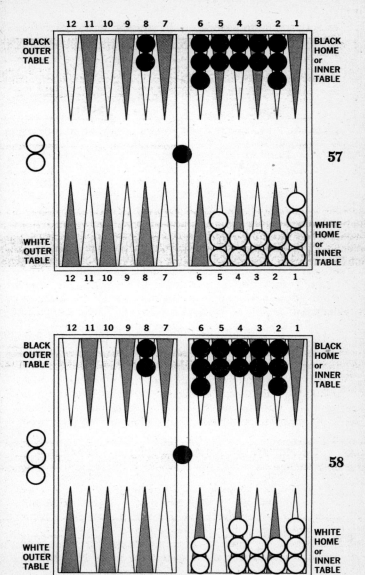

57

58

you get around to bearing off. In positions of this kind, the chances are that you will have to give him a shot (leave a blot) sooner or later. The stakes are high: you are likely to win a gammon if you don't get hit, but you are likely to lose the game if you do. Unlike the closed-board situation, your opponent must play while you are bringing in your men.

If you can force him to break his own board, you can stand being hit, so one thing you may want to do is delay your own movement.

In the position shown in Diagram 59 you are delighted to roll 2–1. This is the smallest roll there is, and it also gives you a chance to pile up four men on your bar point. This makes it impossible for you to move a 6, so you can hold your position quite a while if you should roll 6s.

Black proceeds to roll 6–1. In this position he also wants to delay himself. Therefore he brings both his men into his home board (he moves the man from his nine to his three point, and the man from his bar point to the six point). Now he doesn't have to move 6s either.

The position shown in Diagram 60 develops a few plays later. White has brought his men in nicely, and black has managed to retain most of his board. White is also in safe position, at least for this one play. He rolls 6–3.

He has to bear off one man from the six point and may either bear a man from the three point or move a man from the five to the two point.

It is usually correct to move an odd man from a high point, but this time the correct play is to bear the man from the three point. In addition to giving you an infinitesimal extra chance to win a gammon, the play is far safer.

Let's assume that black does not roll a 6 and is thus still able to keep both his men on your one point. Now let's see what can happen to white at his next turn.

If white has borne a man from the three point, as we suggest, he will be left with two men on the six point and three men on the five point. He will leave a blot on his next move only if he rolls double 6 or 6–5.

However, let's see what would happen if white had moved a man from the five to the two point. Now he will

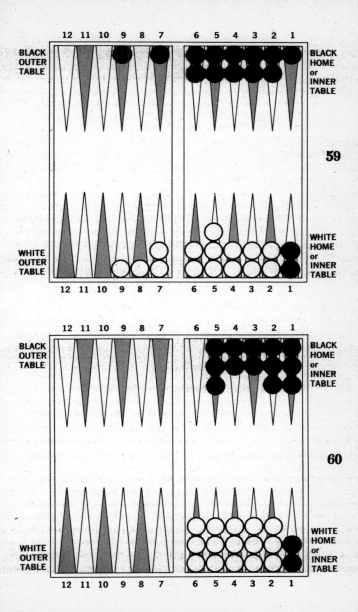

have two men each on the six and five points. If he rolls 5-4, he will have to expose one of those two men on the five point; and if he rolls 6–5, something much worse will happen to him: he will have to expose men on both the five and six points.

Therefore, there is no question about the superiority of bearing off the man from the three point. You should make it a definite rule, in this and similar cases, to try to play in such a manner that if you throw a bad number you will leave only one man exposed rather than two.

Nevertheless, keep in mind that the general rule is to move off your high points and to pile your men up on the lower points.

Another general point to keep in mind is that the safer play in backgammon is sometimes ignored when a gammon is involved. We'll now discuss an example where even the greatest experts might well disagree on the best play. Look at Position 61; you roll double 2.

An optimistic player will bear off four men from the two point, saying to himself, "I have a good chance to win a gammon. True, I may have to give a shot the very next roll, but I may still win the game even if my blot is hit."

A more conservative man will move his two men from the five to the three point, and his two men on the four point to the two point. He will say to himself, "If I am lucky, I may still win a gammon. I won't have to give a shot on the next roll, and I'm quite likely never to give a shot. Playing this way, I can generally take my winnings down to the bank."

We would make the conservative play, but we wouldn't criticize anyone making the liberal play.

## Holding One Point in Your Opponent's Board

This situation is what might be called a partial back game. You can wait with just one point in your possession. Until your opponent manages to get all of his men past that one point, you will still have a chance to get a shot at him. Hit his blot and you may win the game.

The higher the number of the point that you hold in his

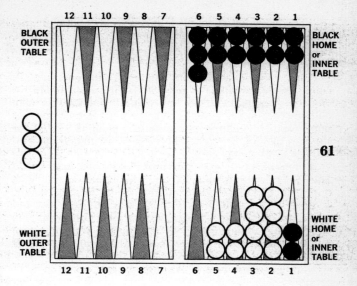

board, the less the chance of your getting that shot. We will not discuss all the plays from each one of his points but will point out that the choice between running and staying isn't always open to you, and that when you do run from a high point be careful not to leave one man in your opponent's board if he has a good chance to swarm on that one blot.

Thus, in Position 62 it is downright silly to run with one man if you happen to roll 6–4. Simply move two men from the black twelve point. You aren't in real danger of being gammoned if you keep your two men on the black four point. On the other hand, if you do run with one man and then black rolls any combination of 4s, 3s, 2s, and 1s, he will hit your blot and make his four point; then you will be in real danger of losing a gammon.

As a matter of fact, in this position you wouldn't even

run with both your men with 6–5. You want to hold that point and play for a shot at one of black's men. You aren't risking a gammon if you stay but have practically no chance to win if you run.

Position 63 is a different matter. Your running-game count (see Chapter 6) is only 86 (represented by 42 for your two men on the black four point, plus 7 for your man on your bar point, and 37 for the twelve men in your home board), while your opponent's count is 77 (32 for the four men on his eight point and 45 for the eleven men in his home board).

If you roll 6–4, you can wait with both men in his home board if you want to, but you shouldn't. Run with one man. Black can point on your blot if he rolls double 4, double 2, double 1, or 4–2. He can hit your blot and go on to safety with 4–3, 4–1, 3–2, or 2–1. Otherwise, you will be able to run with your last man at your next turn with almost an even chance to win the running game. If

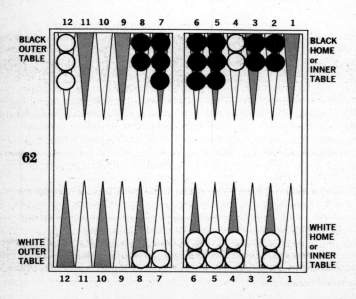

62

you wait, you materially hurt your running-game chances, since you will still have to bring those two back men around the board before you get around to bearing any men off.

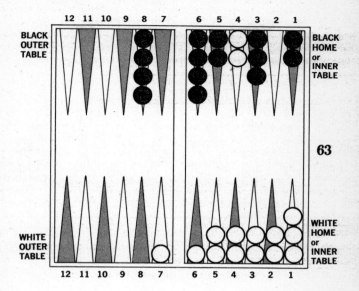

Position 64 arose because you held the black three point early, later had a couple of blots hit, and did not roll any 3s to bring those men back into the board. You have no chance in a running game and little chance to avoid a gammon unless you can hit a blot. Your best strategy is to get two of those four men out of the black inner board and move them around the outer board as fast as you can, but you also want to keep two men on that three point in the faint hope that a shot will materialize. There is no chance of getting one immediately, but if black rolls badly he may not be able to pass your road block without leaving a blot.

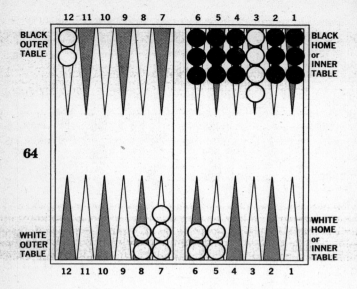

## Holding Your Opponent's One Point

This is the classic partial-back-game position. You don't really get into it from choice. It is usually the result of just managing to make the one point while your opponent has been filling the rest of his board, or the result of your back men having never left the one point at all.

The late Buddy Simonson, who was one of the greatest of all backgammon players, used to remark that if he managed to make his opponent's one point in an otherwise hopeless position, "I'm in the game to the finish." What he meant was that as long as he could hold that point he would have a chance to hit a blot, and if he hit that blot he would have a chance to win the game.

This is absolutely true. We have seen games won after an opponent had borne off fourteen men. Not that we

140

want to play against just one man as a steady diet, but "where there's life, there's hope," so as long as you hold that one point you have a chance.

If you have more than two men on that one point, the extra men are just liabilities for you. Each extra man just increases your chance of losing a gammon or a backgammon, so try to get all but two men off that point. If you can move an odd man to another point in black's board where it represents an additional threat against black's men, do so. Otherwise, just get those extra men out of the black inner board as fast as you can.

Look at Position 65. You roll 6-3. Use the 3 to move a man to the black four point and the 6 to bring the man on the black twelve point to your bar point.

You may be gammoned; you may even be backgammoned; but if black's next roll happens to be 6-5, he will have to leave blots on his six and five points and you will

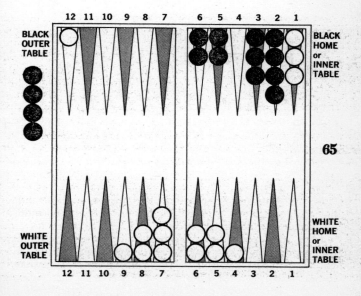

141

then be a favorite to win the game, since you will hit at least one blot if your next roll is anything except double 6, double 3, or 6–3.

When you have just two men on the one point, it usually pays to keep them there. In Position 66 if you rolled 6–1 it would be silly to move one man out of the black home board, and suicidal to split and move one man to the black two point. The first procedure would make it pos-

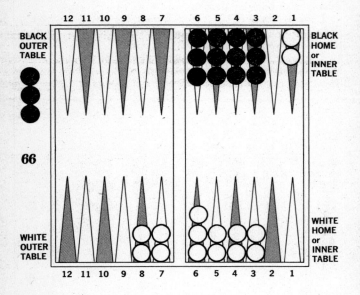

sible for black to point on your blot with any roll that did not include an ace or a 6; the second procedure would leave him *two* blots to point on.

Other positions aren't as extreme as this one, but the general rule should be to hold two men on that one point *as long as your opponent has men on two or more points in his board.*

In Position 67 you also roll 6–1; you have an automatic split situation with the 1. Split those two back men (move one to the two point), and black will almost surely have to give you a double shot. He will even have to leave *three* blots if he rolls 3–2.

You won't get into positions like 67 often, but you will frequently come down to the classic situation in which all your opponent's remaining men are on his two point. Then it becomes essential for you to leave only one man on the one point. If you have two men on the one point and he rolls 6–1, 5–1, 4–1, 3–1, or 2–1, he just bears off one man and doesn't play the 1 at all. If you have only one man there, on the other hand, he must hit him with the 1, and thereby leave you a return shot on his one point.

When you are down to two men on the black one point and can run with one or both men, don't do so if you have little or no chance to save a gammon. *Do* run if you

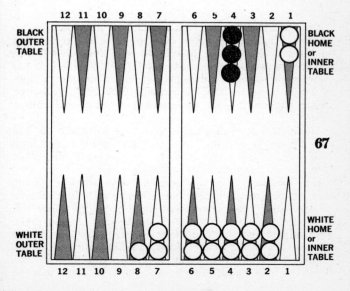

67

143

see that you have a good chance to prevent a gammon and thus escape with only the loss of a regular game.

When you're down to one man on that black one point, you should almost always run if by doing so you expect to save the gammon. It is very sporting to wait around and hope for the best, but it is better financially to keep your losses down.

When you get down to this classic position—having all remaining black men on his two point while you have one man on his one point—your final problem will be whether to make a last-ditch stand in a desperate effort to win the game, or to run and at least save the backgammon.

Suppose black is down to just two men on his two point. Most players wait and hope, but this is silly. Just run and concede the gammon. Let's figure the whole thing out.

Black will win a triple (backgammon) if he rolls anything except 6–1, 5–1, 4–1, 3–1, or 2–1. In other words, the odds are twenty-six to ten, or almost three to one, in favor of his backgammoning you.

And he may still win that triple game even if he makes a bad roll. You might come back with a roll of 3–2 and be unable either to hit him or to get out of his home board.

How do you gain by waiting? Only if he makes one of those ten bad rolls and you then roll an ace, allowing you to hit his blot coming in off the bar. You have eleven chances to get an ace (double 1, 6–1, 5–1, 4–1, 3–1, 2–1); thus, your chance of gaining is represented by the product of 10/36 times 11/36. This is exactly 110/1296, and while it can happen, the odds are more than ten to one against you.

Thus, if you wait desperately, you are going to lose about three times out of four, and gain less than one time in eleven. *So don't wait with one man on black's one point when he has only two men on his two point.*

The situation is just the opposite when black has three men on his two point. He has only five rolls (any double except aces) that can backgammon you; one other roll that won't leave you a shot (double aces: he hits your man on the one point and bears off his man, then moves the two remaining men on his two point down to the one point); and thirty rolls that *do* give you a shot at him. Twenty of these rolls just give you a single shot, while ten

144

of them (6–1, 5–1, 4–1, 3–1, and 2–1) will give you a double shot.

In addition, if he does leave two blots and you can pick both of them up, you become a distinct favorite to win the game. *So wait with one man on black's one point when he has three men on that two point.*

When he has exactly four men on the two point, you should wait one roll if you have no chance to save the gammon by running, but run in case you have *some chance* of saving the gammon. Remember, if you run and he then rolls an ace, he will probably need three rolls to get all his men off. And if your man on his one point is your only man not already in your home board, three rolls should give you time to bring him around and take a man off, thereby saving the gammon.

When he has more than four men on his two point, you should run and save the gammon if you can; otherwise wait and hope for a shot at him.

# 10

# THE BACK GAME

There was once a day in backgammon when everyone was supposed to play safe. Whenever you exposed a blot and it was hit, you lost potential running-game ground, and the theory was that you simply could not afford these setbacks.

As the game has developed in more recent years, we have seen this safety-first policy almost completely abandoned in favor of a policy of *taking a chance to gain in position, and never mind about the running game until you get to it.*

We know that some modern experts tend to carry this too far. A winning player should always keep the running-game possibilities in mind. He doesn't have to know exactly how he stands, but he should certainly be aware of whether he is well ahead, a little ahead, about even, a little behind, or way behind.

If he's ahead, he should try to disengage his men from his opponent's men and run. If he's a little behind, he should try to maintain contact while keeping his men in such position that he can start disengagement if he begins to outroll his opponent. If he's way behind, he may plan for a semi-back game.

In a semi-back game the man who is behind will gain possessi⟨ ⟩ of his opponent's four or five point, both as an anc⟨ ⟩ a threat against the last men that his opponent ⟨ ⟩ to his home board.

⟨ ⟩ ⟨g⟩ame may develop directly, or from a semi-
⟨ ⟩ ⟨ta⟩king two points in your opponent's home
⟨ ⟩ a back game. You have a classic back

game when you hold his one and three points or one and two points. These are the best pairs of points to hold.

The "nothing game" is a poor relation of the back game. In a nothing game you hold two fine points in your opponent's board—but unfortunately you have been forced to advance your other men so far forward that they are concentrated on your one, two, and three points. Therefore, it won't do you any real good to hit a blot when you get your eventual shot with your back men. Your opponent will have no trouble bringing that blot right back in and around to his home board.

Holding three points in your opponent's board gives you a super-back game. It will prove almost impossible for your opponent to bring his men to full safety. The fly in the ointment here is that you have only nine forward men left, and you are therefore going to have great difficulty in deploying them satisfactorily.

Position 68 illustrates a nothing game. You hold the black one and two points, but you don't hold your own five and six points, and barring a miracle you won't ever make them. It is most unlikely that you will win this game, and the best you can realistically hope for is to be able to avoid a gammon.

Position 69 illustrates a good back game. You can ruin it by rolling a couple of big doubles right away, but otherwise your front-game position will be so good that when you hit a blot you will be able to double and force your opponent to give up. And, of prime importance, your back position is so good that you are a favorite to get a couple of shots and hit at least one blot. Of course you may also wind up being gammoned. This is true of all back games. *A good luck game will win over half the time, but when it loses it is very likely to lose a gammon.*

Therefore, don't get into back games for the sheer joy and excitement of playing them. *Get into back games only because you have no better alternative.*

Also, bear in mind that once you get started on a back game it is up to you to get far enough back so that if you get to hit a blot late in the game, you will have a good enough home board to stop that man from coming right around the board. Therefore, *once you have made two*

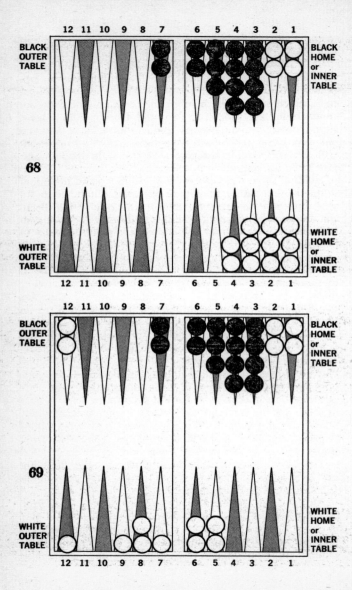

*points in your opponent's board, you should plan to ex-pose other men and get them hit in order to delay your-self and slow up the advance of your front men.* You don't want your men to get piled up on your first few points, which would give you a nothing game. Place these new blots in spots where your opponent won't be able to refuse to hit them.

Conversely, when your opponent starts into a back game, you should not help him develop it. Don't keep hitting his blots for the pleasure of sending extra men back to the bar. Make him move his advanced men so far forward that he will get into a nothing-game position rather than into a satisfactory back game.

Now let's see how a typical back game develops. Position 70 was reached as follows: black started with 4–2 and made his four point. We rolled 5–2 and moved two men from the black twelve point to our eight and eleven points.

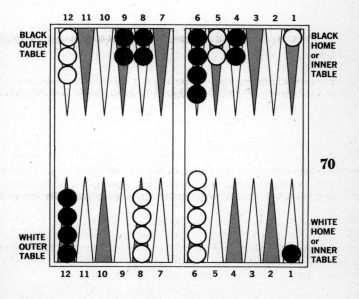

Black rolled 6–4 and hit the blot on our eleven point. We rolled 5–4 and made the black five point, with one man from the black one point and our man on the bar. Black then rolled 5–4 and made his nine point, with the man on our eleven point and a man on our twelve point.

We are already well behind in a potential running game. Black has rolled 4–2, 6–4, and 5–4, for a total of 25 pips (points) and has moved forward with all of them. We have rolled 5–2 and 5–4 for a total of 16, but lost 14 pips when our blot was hit, so that our forward progress is a net of only 2 pips.

Furthermore, black has a better position. He holds four points in his inner and outer boards and has liberated one of his two back men. We just hold everything we started with except for the black one point, and we have made the black five point—our only ray of sunshine.

Our first plan is to utilize that five point, both as a base of operations and as a threat against black's men that still have to move across his outer board. If we roll a 4, we may reinforce that five point; otherwise we will keep that extra man on the black one point as a further threat.

Suppose for a moment that we proceed to roll 6–5. We aren't far enough behind to warrant any play except to bring our back man to safety at the black twelve point. We would do this, and we would probably be in an ordinary middle game from then on.

On the other hand, if we roll a very low number we will want to try to do something about improving our home board. In fact, we roll 2–1, and our correct play is to move a man from our eight point to our five point.

If black rolls a 4, 3–1, or double 2, he will hit that blot, but we won't mind. We will have a fourth man back and be ready to develop a back game. Black could also hit us if he rolled double 1, but a good player wouldn't. He would much prefer to move the two men from his nine point to his bar point.

Black actually rolls 5–4. He hits our blot with the 4 and brings a man from our twelve point to reinforce his eight point. This produces Position 71.

We roll another 2–1. Strangely enough, this is now a good roll. We have any number of ways to play it, and there is no absolutely best way. There *is* one worst way to

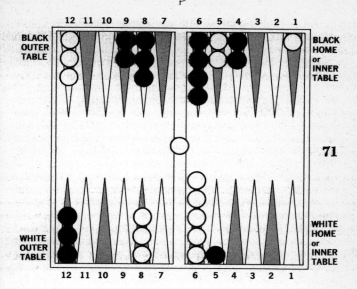

play it, which is to bring that man on the bar up to the black three point. This gains nothing for us and leaves a man exposed to all sorts of deadly combination rolls. The only "advantage" of this play is that black is likely to double us, and if we like to gamble with the worst of it, we can take the double and may be lucky enough to pull out. We will be more likely to wind up being gammoned, but some players who don't care about money don't seem to mind that.

Another bad way to play it is to come in on the one point and move a man from our eight point to our six point. This play merely serves to hurt our forward-game position.

The good plays at our disposal are: (a) make the black two point; (b) come in on the black two point and hit the blot on our five point; (c) make the black one point and move a man to our four point; and (d) make the black one point and expose a blot on our eleven point.

We wouldn't quarrel with any of these four moves. In a chouette (see Chapter 12), if the captain suggested one of them, we would say something like, "Don't care in the slightest." However, we do have our own order of merit here. The poorest of the four, we feel, is play (a): we would rather hold the one point than the two point.

Play (b) is best for the purpose of getting a fifth man back and thereby delaying our forward movement some more: black may be forced to hit that blot on our five point. The play's weakness is that we have left too many blots scattered around our home board and have not established our second back-game point yet.

Play (c) does give us that valuable extra back-game point that we need, but dropping a man on our four point does not help us accomplish our other objective of slowing up our forward movement.

Play (d) gives us that important one point, and also may accomplish our second objective; we want to get another man back in the black inner board and work our way into a real back game. We aren't quite in one now because, unless we roll very small numbers, we won't be able to hold our two points in the black board. But give us a fifth man back and we will simply put him into position to be hit again, and we will then be able to hold our back position.

So we select (d), bringing us to Position 72.

Let's shift our viewpoint for a moment and go over to the black side of the game. He knows that we are trying to develop a back game, and if he is a good player, he won't cooperate with us.

He can hit that blot on our eleven point if he rolls double 6, double 2, 6–5, 6–4, 6–3, 6–2, 6–1, 5–1, or 4–2. His correct plays with these rolls are:

*Double 6.* Hit the blot, and move the three men on the white twelve point to his bar point.

*Double 2.* Make his bar point with the two men on his nine point; then move the man from the white five point to the white nine point, to tempt white (us) to hit him.

*6–5 and 6–4.* Move the man from our five point without hitting the blot. He will be in safety on the black nine point after 6–5, and exposed on the black ten point after 6–4.

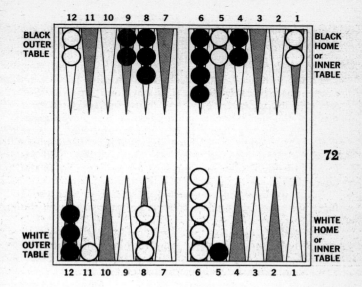

*6–3.* He should move from our five point to his eleven point. In this case, he cannot play the 3 first, so he is forced to hit our blot; but he has no better play.

*6–2* and *6–1.* He should make his bar point. In the case of 6–2, this leaves a blot (on his nine point), but black shouldn't care.

*5–1* and *4–2.* Hit our blot. Again, there is no better play.

You may wonder why we haven't suggested that black should double at this stage of the game. Clearly he has an advantage! The trouble is that the game has a long way to go, and experience will teach you that doubling a potential back game too early is a losing proposition. And right now, if black did double we have a very sound basis for accepting.

There are two reasons why we would be able to take the double: first, black has a lot of work to do before he

153

can get around to bearing off; second, we are likely to get several chances to hit blots before black is safe in his home board.

Resuming the game, let's say black gets a good roll, 6–1, and uses it to make his bar point. We now have some pretty good possible return rolls but come up with 5–2 and can find no better play than to use our two remaining men on the black twelve point to make our eleven point and reinforce our eight point. Black now has a good moment to double us, and we should refuse. We are not going to be able to maintain our back position, and we should therefore take our one-unit loss and get on to the next game.

Could we have played that 5–2 in some way that would leave ourselves in a good enough position to accept the double? Yes!

We could have made the insane-looking play of moving a man from the black twelve point to the white eight point and a man from the white six point to the white four point. This would produce Position 73.

In so doing, we are making it very hard for black to get around the board without hitting a blot and thus giving us the back game we've been trying for. We are also starting to make another point in our inner board and, while we may wind up being gammoned, we now also have an excellent chance of pulling the game out of the fire.

As we mentioned, you'll find that this is standard with almost all back games. You either win the game or wind up being gammoned.

Black now doubles, and we accept. Then black rolls 3–1 and can find nothing better to do than to hit our blot on his twelve point and then go on to his nine point. We roll 6–5 and simply bring the man on the bar out to the black eleven point. We have delayed ourselves a trifle, and still have two blots that he may be forced into hitting.

A few rolls later we reach Position 74. It is black's roll, and his men are nicely placed, but we still hold his one and five points.

Black rolls 6–2—an embarrassingly good roll. He has two ways to play it. One is to make his two point. The other is to give up his nine point in order to reinforce his

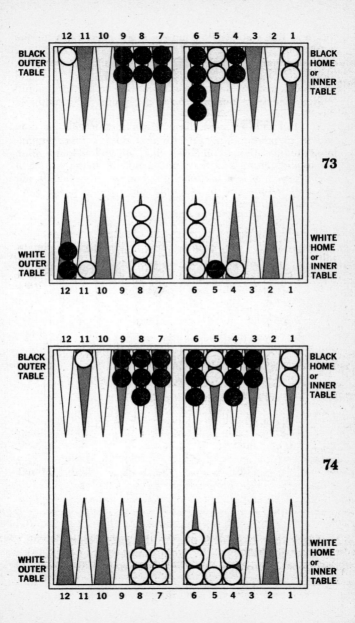

bar and three points. We have a slight preference for the latter play, but we would not object if our partners in a chouette wanted to make the other move. Anyway, black decides to make his two point, and we then roll 5–1 and move our man on the black eleven point to our nine point, and a man from our six to our five point. This produces Position 75.

If black can get past those white obstructions, he may win a gammon; if he gets hit and doesn't make an immediate sensational comeback shot, we will redouble him, he should refuse, and the game would be over. In fact, if black now makes a bad enough shot, we may decide our position is too good to redouble and play to win a gammon for ourselves!

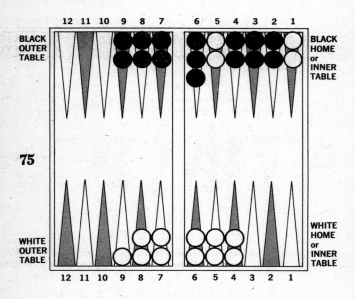

Black rolls 4–3 and is safe for this roll at least. This is a bad roll for him since he has to move two men from his bar point (or else leave a blot, far worse). We then roll

6–5 and give up the white eight point to make the white three point (with the man on our nine point and one of those on our eight point). Our reception committee is still ready!

Black rolls another 4–3, and now he has to give us a shot. He can't play 4 from the nine point or 3 from the eight point and can only afford to move one man from his six point, so he makes his best play by moving a man from his nine to his two point. We are now in Position 76.

You may wonder why he exposed on the nine point instead of the eight point. The reason is that this play exposes the blot to any 4, a 6–2, or double 2, a total of fourteen shots. If he had exposed on the eight point he could have been hit by any 3, a 2–1, or 6–1, a total of fifteen shots.

This Position 76 is typical of a back game well played by both sides. White will win if he hits that blot on the black nine point, unless black makes the miracle comeback

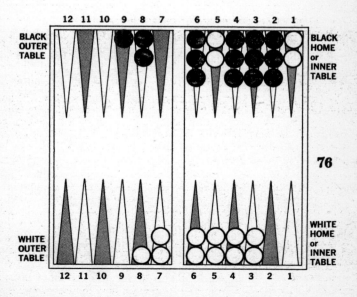

shot of 6–2. The fact that white has now been given this one shot fully justifies his earlier acceptance of black's double. Even if white now misses, there is an excellent chance that he will get at least one more shot later on.

Why did black double when he did? The answer is that black might have brought his men past our back-game points and gammoned us without giving us a shot at him. He doubled with that hope in mind. We accepted with the hope of developing a position such as this one.

## Some Back-Game Positions

In Position 77 black is playing a back game. You roll 5–3 and are going to break either from your nine point (arriving at Position 78) or from your bar point (Position 79).

Which play should you make? Position 78 looks mighty pretty. You still hold five points in a row. But then the

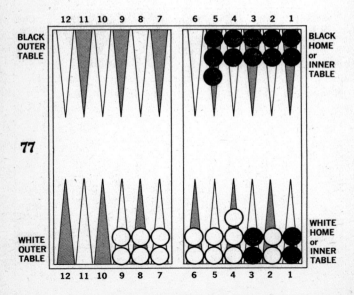

158

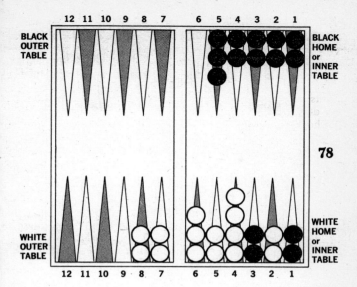

only really bad rolls for black would be those with a 6, which would force him to run from your three point, in which case you might hurt him badly (double 6 would not, of course, hurt him as much). If he doesn't roll a 6, he will be forced to move in his inner board, but if he rolls double 5, 5–4, 5–3, 5–2, or 5–1, he won't be able to play the five at all and will maintain his board. Then if you roll 6–5, you'll have to move one man each from your eight and bar points and thus be exposed to any 4, 5, or 6, a total of twenty-seven rolls.

Position 79 doesn't look as pretty, but it is a trifle more sound. To begin with, black will have to break one of the points in your board if he rolls double 4, 5–4, or any 6, a total of fourteen rolls. In Position 78 he has only eleven rolls that would force him to give up a point in your board. In addition, if black does maintain the *status quo* and you roll 6–5, you will still have to leave two blots, but you will

159

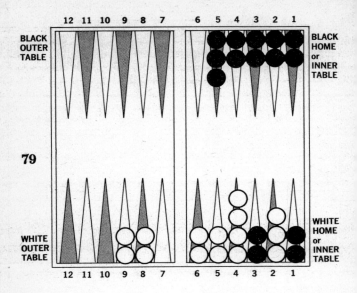

be exposed to only twenty-four rolls instead of twenty-seven.

Thus, we have a slight preference for getting to Position 79.

In Position 80 your back game isn't going too well because you haven't been able to delay the movement of your forward men enough to create a sure thing for yourself if you should hit one of your opponent's blots. You have one of the two classic back-game holdings: the black one and two points. Black has his men placed excellently, however, and unless his next roll is 6–5 or double 4 you aren't going to get an immediate shot at him.

You roll a very satisfactory 2–1. You could retain your five-point board by moving the third man on your five point to your two point, but the correct play is to give up your six point and move those two men to your four and five points. This looks a trifle silly: why give up a point when you don't have to? But the reason that this is a very good play is that you want to hold as much of a board as you can. You aren't likely to hit a blot at your next turn or even the turn after. If you attempt to hold your six point, you will have to move a man with any 5; but by giving up the six point you are delaying yourself, because you won't be able to play a 5 at all and will be quite likely to hold your five, four, three, and two points for a long time.

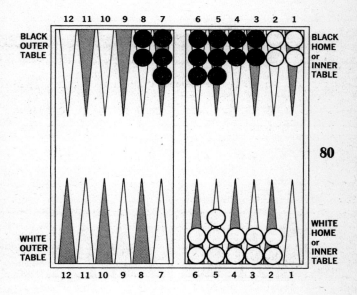

In Position 81 black doesn't really have a back game since he holds only one point in the white board, but he is so far behind in the running game (151 to 93) that you are not going to lose the game unless he can hit a blot. You proceed to roll 5–4. Your possible plays are to move two men from your eleven point to your bar point and six point, or two from your ten point to your six and five points.

The correct play is to move the two men from your ten point. The reason is that unless you are quite lucky you will later have to leave a blot. If you maintain your ten point and later leave a blot there, it will be exposed to any 6 (a direct shot) plus some combination shots. But if you move as we suggest, and thus maintain your eleven point instead, and later are forced to leave a blot there, it will be exposed only to 7, a combination shot.

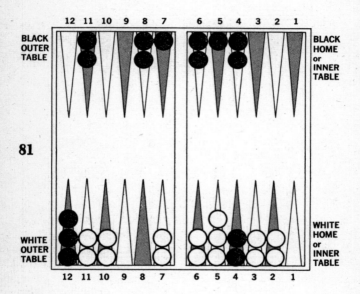

81

In Position 82 your men are placed exactly the same and black has the same two men on your four point, but his other thirteen men are all well advanced in his home board. Your count is still 93, but his is only 71, so he is ahead of you in the running game. His lead is not much since you expect to start bearing off first, but all in all he is a trifle ahead. Your game plan should be to hamper those two men on your four point as much as possible, and to hit one of them if you can.

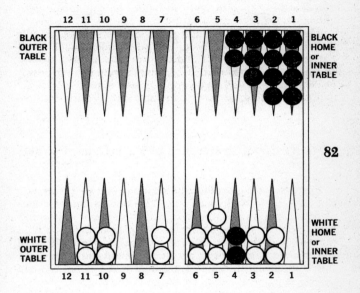

Thus, if you roll that same 5–4, you should break your eleven point and keep the men on the ten point to block 6s. If black rolls double 6, he won't be able to move at all; if he rolls 6–3, 6–2, or 6–1, he will not be able to play the 6, and can move only the 1, 2, or 3 uselessly in his home board. If he rolls double 5 or double 4, he will get both men out, but there is nothing you can do against either of those two rolls in any case. If he rolls 6–5, 6–4, any 5, or any 4, he will be forced to move one of those back men out, whereupon the other man left on your four point will be exposed to direct 6s, 3s, 2s, and 1s. You should hit that man even though you may have to leave a blot in the process. The odds are that he won't hit you back, and it is essential that you delay him. Note that 5–1, 4–2, and 4–1 are "death" shots for black. He must move one man out of your board so that both those back men will be exposed. You are likely to pick both up before he can escape with either.

There is one more thing to consider here. If black rolls 5–4, his best play will be to bring both men out. He will be exposed to direct 2s and 1s, but that is only twenty numbers out of thirty-six. If he leaves a man in your board, he will be exposed to every number except double 5, double 4, or 5–4, or thirty-two shots out of thirty-six.

## The Order of Preference of Back-Game Points

There are ten possible combinations of two points you can have for a back game (i.e., the various combinations of points one, two, three, four, and five in your opponent's home board). In the classic back-game position you hold the one and three or the one and two points. We have found almost unanimous agreement among experts about this, and almost the same agreement that holding the one and three points is slightly superior to the one and two.

After this, we couldn't agree between ourselves about the order of preference of the other eight possibilities. To try to settle our own argument, we asked some of the world's best players for their opinions. To our amazement, no two of our group came up with the same order of preference!

Our group of experts included Barclay Cooke, the dean of New York's Racquet Club players, and his son Walter, who together easily form the best father-and-son pair in the game; Tim Holland, winner of three major tournaments; Porter Ijams, who has been runner-up three times in major tournaments and consistently is among the best players; Tobias Stone, one of the great bridge players, who

164

has also won a major backgammon tournament; Paul Miller of Los Angeles, one of the best players on the West Coast; and Stephen Raphael of London, who has long been one of the best, if not *the* best, of Britain's players.

We will not list each one's preferences, but instead have formed a consensus:

| | |
|---|---|
| Best points | one and three |
| Second best | one and two |
| Third best | two and three |
| Fourth best | two and four |
| Fifth best | three and four |
| Sixth best | one and four |
| Seventh best | three and five |
| Eighth best | four and five |
| Next to worst | two and five |
| Worst | one and five |

If you wonder why the consensus favors the one and three points over the one and two points, it is a matter of timing.

When you hold the one and two points your opponent will come to a position in which he won't be able to play either a 5 or a 6, and if he starts rolling those numbers he will be able to hold his position, while you may have to break up your own home board. When you hold the one and three points he will have more room to move and therefore will be less able to hold his position, so your shot or shots are more likely to come while you still have your home board in good shape.

It is interesting to note that there was one conspicuous dissent to our consensus that the five point was the worst back-game point. Stephen Raphael, our British expert, was the first player to build his entire game plan around the two five points. He wanted yours for defense and his own for attack, but since Stephen is by nature conservative he went for his opponent's five point as first objective.

Then if he wanted to go into a back game, he would simply add another point and play a sort of all-purpose game in which he could if he wished move from the five point, save the other point for purposes of harassment, and have a good chance of avoiding a gammon in case a successful shot failed to materialize.

Our other experts believe in going all out with their back games and playing to win, on the theory of "damn the torpedoes, full speed ahead."

*Remember, in any case, that the back game is regarded by most of the world's top players as an all-out gamble, leading either to a win or to being gammoned.*

# 11

## UNUSUAL PLAYS

Some of the following unusual plays occur frequently and are classified as "unusual" merely because they seem to violate the general principles of play.

One of these is hitting a man on your one point in an effort to keep your opponent from improving his forward position too much.

Look at Position 83. You don't have much of a game here and proceed to roll 5–2, which helps matters very little. You have to use the 2 to bring in your man from the bar. Suppose you then use the 5 to make the conservative play of moving a man from the black twelve to your eight point. If black hasn't doubled already, he will double now, and you should refuse. Twenty-seven rolls (anything except double 5, 5–3, 5–1, 4–3, or 4–1) will allow him to make either the bar point or the four point. Furthermore, 4–1 lets him hit both your men; and he has satisfactory ways to play the other possible rolls. Thus you are too likely to be gammoned if you take the double and play on.

So, to gain time and avoid being doubled, you should not make the conservative play. Instead, use the 5 to hit his blot on your one point. This play buys time for you since he will have to play part of his next roll in your home board. If he rolls 6–1 or 4–1, he will hit your blot on your one point and use the 6 or the 4 to hit the blot you just left on his two point coming in, thereby leaving you with two men off the board. If he rolls 5–1, he will make the same kind of play but this time will hit your man on his one point with the 5. Double 1, double 2, or double 3 will also be very good rolls for him. That makes a total of nine really good rolls, which does not represent a doubling advantage for him.

This play may even pay an unexpected dividend: black may roll double 6, double 4, or 6–4, and forfeit his whole roll.

You are going to have many similar situations where your best or even your only satisfactory defensive play is to hit a man in your board and keep your opponent busy.

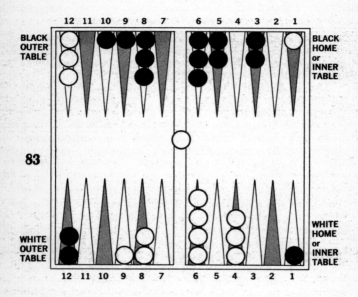

83

Position 84 illustrates the possibility of hitting a man on your one point as an attacking play. You roll 4–1. You could play it quietly by making your nine point, but the best way to play it is to hit both his blots with one of the men on your six point. Here is an analysis of his possible replies:

Number of rolls that enable him to bring
both men in and hit your blot         7

| Number of rolls that enable him to bring both men in but miss your blot | 9 |
| Number of rolls that enable him to bring one man in and hit your blot | 4 |
| Number of rolls that enable him to bring one man in but miss your blot | 12 |
| Number of rolls that keep both his men on the bar | 4 |
| Total possible rolls | 36 |

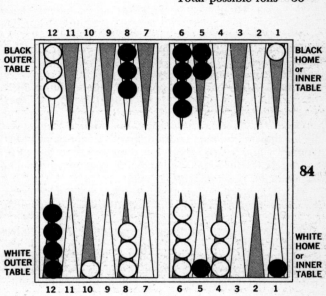

84

His only good rolls are double 1, double 2, double 3, and double 5, and not one of these hurts you very much. With double 1 he points on your blot on your one point, and makes his bar point; with double 2 he makes your two point and his four point; with double 3 he makes both three points; with double 5 he enters both men and keeps them going to hit the blot on your ten point.

None of his other thirty-two rolls are much good to him. The twelve that enable him to bring one man in without hitting your blot leave you a definite favorite in the game, while if he rolls 6–6, 6–4, or double 4, and fails to bring either man in off the bar, you will have an excellent moment to double him, and he should refuse.

Now let's take a detailed look at the plays he could make if you had made the inferior play of making your nine point:

*Double 1.* He makes his bar point, moves one man from his six to his five point, and brings the man on your one point to your two point.

*Double 2.* He makes his four point and your five point— a very strong play.

*Double 3.* He makes his bar point.

*Double 4.* He has a choice of any number of excellent plays. They're all so good that we need not discuss their relative merits.

*Double 5.* He makes his one and three points, leaving you with a man on the bar and himself with a four-point board. You are going to need a very good return roll to stay alive.

*Double 6.* He makes his bar point, and brings the man on white five point to his eight point.

*6–5.* He runs from white's five point to his nine point. He doesn't want to leave that man on your five point to be hit.

*6–4.* He has three fair plays. He can make the white five point and expose a blot on his bar point; we favor this move since if you don't then roll a 6, 5–1, 4–2, or double 3, it will be his game. The other two plays are to run from your five to his ten point (second best, in our judgment), or to make his two point (third best).

*6–3.* Run from the white five point to his own eleven point.

*6–2.* Make the white bar point.

*5–4.* Use the 4 to make the white five point, and reinforce his own eight point.

*5–3.* Make his three point.

*5–2.* Run from the white five point to white twelve point.

*5–1.* Not a good roll. He should either hit your blot on

his one point with the 5 (*a defensive play to keep you busy*) and move the 1 anywhere, or he should play from white five to your ten point and move from his six to his five point.

*4–3.* Make the white five point, and move a man from the white twelve point to his ten point.

*4–2.* Two good alternates: he can make his four point, or he can make the white five point and move a man to his eleven point.

*4–1.* Make your white five point, and move a man from his six to his five point.

*3–2.* Not a good roll. There are several ways to play it. We have a very slight preference for moving from the white five point to the white ten point.

*3–1.* Make the white five point.

*2–1.* Not good. His best play is to move his man on the white one point to the three point, and a man on his six point to his five point.

Make careful note of the great difference between the two ways you could play the 4–1 in Position 84. If you make the aggressive play we recommend, your opponent then has four good rolls, sixteen nondescript rolls, twelve bad rolls, and four disastrous rolls. If you make the conservative play, he has only eight poor rolls (6–4, 5–1, 3–2, and 2–1), while his other twenty-eight rolls are either good or very good.

Position 85 developed after black made his two point early and then tried unsuccessfully to escape with one of his back men. You hit that man and have continued to contain both back men in your inner board. You also doubled the stake some time back, and he made a mistake and accepted. You are now playing to win a gammon, and you roll 5–3.

You can play absolutely safe by moving two men from your bar and five points to your two point, but this would be a bad move indeed. In the first place, it will greatly reduce your chance to win a gammon since black will then be able to play his full move. In the second place, it will pile men up on your two point and weaken your whole position. So you quickly decide against this play and plan to take some chance.

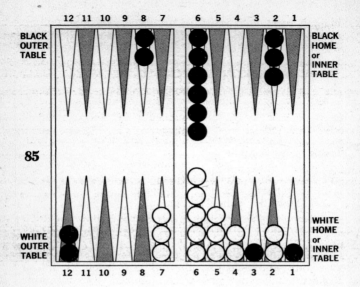

Two possibilities are: (a) hit his blot on the three point with the 3, and move from your bar point to your two point with the 5; and (b) hit his blot on the one point with the 5, and move from your bar point to the four point with the 3.

Neither of these moves represents any real risk of the game, and either one will lead to a gammon if black fails to get in on his first roll. But if he comes in and makes a point in your board, your good chance to win a gammon will have disappeared. He will hold that point as an anchor and move his other men around the board without disturbance. If he gets really lucky, he may build up a good board for himself, hit a blot if you have to leave one in the end game, and come out a winner. Most of the time he will merely succeed in averting the gammon.

If he hits your blot when he comes in, he will probably leave two blots in your board and his position will still be desperate. The two points he holds in his board aren't likely to annoy you, and you will keep on hitting his blots whenever you can.

Of these two plays (b) is the better, but there is a third play that most experts would make. That play is to hit both his blots with men from your six point. You still aren't risking the game, but you are making the outstanding play to win a gammon. If he fails to bring either man in, you are almost sure to fill your board quickly and romp home. If he brings one man in, he will still have a man on the bar and may never get that second man back in.

Only 3–1, double 3, or double 1 will do him any good, and you can afford this slight risk.

Sometimes you may use the double bump as a two-way measure. In Position 86 you roll 3–1. Your position is a poor one and calls for desperate measures. You already have the start of a back game, but you want to get farther back or to develop your forward game quickly. You use your 1 to hit the blot on your five point. You might use

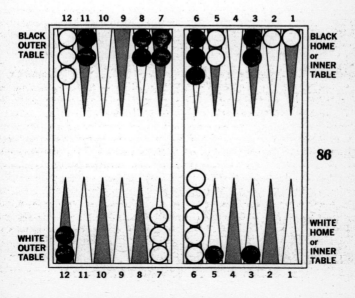

the 3 to move from the black two point to the five point, but instead you should use it to hit the blot on your three point with another man from your six point.

If black fails to hit either of your blots, you are in excellent shape to start making up a good board. If he hits them, you will then have extra men back and will be able to hold a back game against him.

## The Unnecessary Exposure

In Position 87 black doubled you a couple of rolls back and has succeeded in completing a prime against your two back men. You proceed to roll 5–4. You have one, and only one, good play here. This is to move the man on your eleven point to your bar point and a man from the black twelve point to your eight point.

You won't be happy if black then rolls a 5, and hits

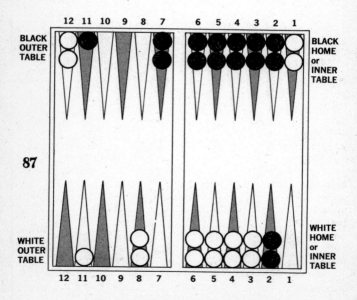

your blot on your bar point, but the game won't be lost. If you fail to enter on his one point for several rolls and he fails to roll another 5 in that same period, you will hold your position while he will have to break first his prime and then his board.

Even if he gets his other man on your two point out and away and hits the blot you have left on his twelve point, you will still be holding the one point in his board and have a chance to win the game if he fails to roll safe numbers.

If he does not roll a 5 on his first roll (and remember that the odds are twenty-five to eleven that he won't) you will have two men in position to complete your own prime. If you succeed in this, since he will be more advanced in his board than you are, the odds are that he will have to break his prime first, whereupon you should win the game easily.

As a matter of minor interest, if instead of a 5 he rolls double 3 or double 4, he will be forced to break his prime then and there, and you would be able to double him immediately.

## Hitting Two Men

*If you can hit two blots left by your opponent you should usually do so.* The reason for this is that you are putting him under considerable pressure. He has to bring them back in, so unless he rolls a playable doublet his next play will be a compulsory one. Even if he does roll a playable doublet, half of his play will be compulsory since he has to use it to bring those two men back into the board.

What makes hitting two blots so strong is that there is a good chance that he won't be able to bring both of those men in on his next roll. Even if you hold just one point in your inner board, the odds in favor of his bringing both men in on one roll are twenty-five to eleven, or just a trifle better than two to one. If you hold two points in your inner board, the odds are five to four *against* his bringing both men in, while if you hold three points, the odds are three to one against him.

Thus, it is almost always good strategy to hit two blots outside your home board. The only exceptions are: (1) you have some other really outstanding play at your disposal; or (2) you have a winning position without hitting them, and don't want to help your opponent into a back game.

Even when you have to leave one blot in your home board in order to bump (hit) two men, it is still pretty good policy to make the bump play. If he hits your blot back you have lost some running-game space, but if he misses (as the odds favor) you have made a substantial gain in position.

The extreme example of the double-bump play occurs when you hit two blots in your home board and leave two blots of your own in doing this. This looks suicidal at first glance. Why ask for trouble? Isn't your opponent favored by the odds to hit at least one of those blots? And doesn't he have some chance of hitting them both?

Of course he's a favorite to hit one, and of course he may be able to hit both. So when should you make this play?

There are two situations when you should. The first, as we noted in discussing Position 86, is when you have the worst of the game and want to try some desperate measure. Maybe he is threatening to develop a very strong position in his home and outer boards. By bumping two men you keep him occupied, bringing them in for at least one roll. Suppose he then hits both your blots? What of it: you have a chance to bring them in and solidify your back-game position.

Position 88 shows the other situation when you should make this play: you are working on a gammon.

You roll 6–4. You must use the 6 to hit his blot on your two point. How should you play the 4?

You can move a man from your eight point to your four point. In this case if black rolls a 2, he comes in, hitting your blot; if he rolls an ace, he makes his one point. In this latter case you are then very unlikely to be able to win a gammon, since he will hold that point indefinitely while moving his other men around the board toward home. He may even win the game at the finish if you have to expose a blot and he hits it. In the other case he has an excellent chance to make either your one or two point with the same end result.

176

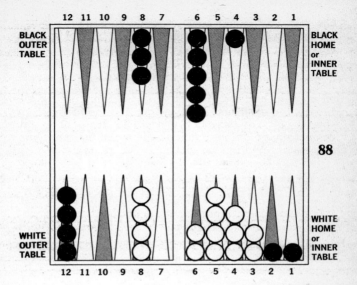

Your better play is to use the 4 to hit the man on your one point. This will put two of his men on the bar while you will have men exposed on your one and two points. If he rolls double 2 or 1, he will succeed in making a point in his board, but his position will still be very bad. If he rolls 2–1, he will also be likely to avert gammon. *But if he rolls anything else, you are almost surely going to gammon him.*

## Advanced Bearing-Off Tactics

In almost all instances, in bearing off you should plan to bear as many men as possible and to spread the men you can't bear off on to empty points. But there are exceptions even here. Suppose you roll double 1 when you have two men each on your one, two, and three points. The normal play is to bear off three men, leaving yourself with one man on the two point and two on the three point. This will almost ensure that you'll be able to end the game in two rolls and is normally the correct play.

But suppose that your opponent's position is such that you are going to get only one more roll. *Now you must find the move that will give you the best chance of getting off on your next roll.* You do this by bearing off just the two men on your one point and moving the two men on your three point to your two point! In this position any doublet except double 1 will get you off; in the other position neither double 1 nor double 2 will get you off.

This example illustrates the fact that your play should be based on how you stand in the game. *When ahead, you should tend to play to guard against bad rolls such as aces; when you're behind, you should try to get yourself in position to get maximum results from doublets.*

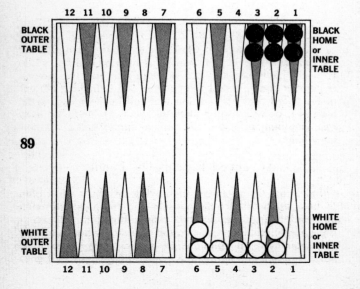

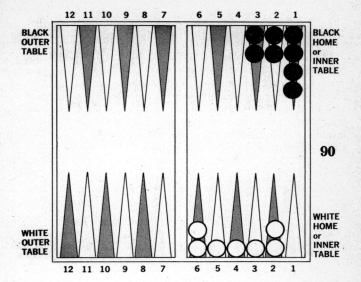

Look at Positions 89 and 90. In each, you roll 6–1. Your correct play in 89 is to move to the position in Diagram 91. Your correct play in 90 is to move to the position shown in Diagram 92.

The reason is that in the first case (Position 89) you calculate that black will be off in three rolls, and *thus you except only two more turns after this one*. By moving a man from the six to the five point, you will be able to bear off four men with either double 5 or double 6.

In the second case (90) you calculate that black needs four rolls to get off, so you will have three more turns; thus, *your plan is to give yourself the best chance to get off in those three turns*. Now you won't need to roll any doubles, and with a man on each point you will be certain to get two men off on your next roll.

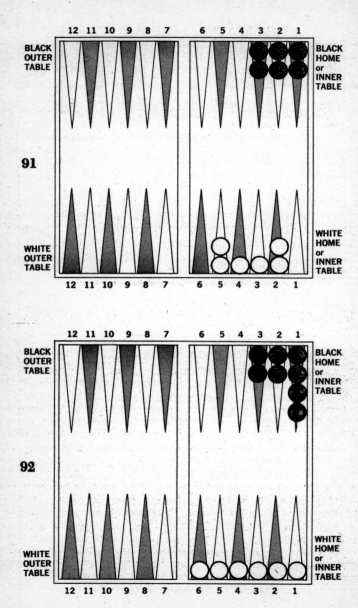

## 12

# CHOUETTE

A chouette is backgammon for more than two people, and is thus a more social form of the game. There can be three, four, five, or even more players.

At the beginning of play all the participants roll one die. The player rolling the highest number is "the man in the box" (or, more simply, "the box"), and he plays against all the others.

The man rolling the second highest number is "captain" of those playing against the box. The third highest roller becomes player number one, the fourth highest player two, and so on. They are the captain's partners and, while they may consult with the captain over the plays, they are bound by his decisions—except that when the man in the box offers a double, each player may accept or reject for himself regardless of what the captain does.

If there are any ties in the opening rolls, the dice are rolled again by the tied men only. The final order of numbers determines the players' positions.

Throughout the session the players maintain a definite order. The winner of each game always becomes the man in the box for the next game. If the captain wins, he takes the box; his opponent goes to the foot of the line, becoming the last player of the opposing team now. Each of the captain's partners moves up a place, so that player number one now becomes captain, and so on. If the box wins, the man in the box remains there, but the losing captain goes to the foot of the line and each of his partners moves forward one place as before.

Any additional players who may join the game come in at the bottom of the line at the start of a new game.

In scoring the game, the man in the box plays against each of his opponents separately. If he wins a one-point game, each of the other players loses one point to him. If he loses, he loses one point to each of them. Thus, if he loses to three players, he loses a total of three times the stake; if he wins, he wins three times the stake.

When the box doubles during a game and the captain gives up, some other player or players may decide to take the double. The senior accepting player then becomes the captain and continues playing the game. If he wins, he gets the box and the others continue their normal order of rotation, except that the losing man in the box takes the foot of the line while the captain who refused the double takes the next to bottom spot. If a man who accepts the double and plays on loses, he does not lose his place in the line. Any player refusing a double has no more interest in the game and may not advise the captain further.

Suppose the box is playing against a captain and players one, two, three, and four, the man in the box doubles, and players two and four are the only ones to accept. If the box wins, player one becomes captain; player two becomes number one, player three becomes number two, player four moves to number three, and the captain goes to number four. If player two, the senior man who took the double, wins, he gets the box; player one, who refused the double, still becomes captain; number three becomes player one; number four becomes player two; the original captain becomes number three; and the losing man in the box becomes number four.

In a chouette, the captain and his partners tend to double rather quickly. The idea is to put money pressure on the man in the box. So the man in the box is likely to be a trifle slow with his doubles, since he must consider potential redoubles. However, somehow or other there usually seems to be a certain chouette intoxication. The same man who doubles very slowly in a two-handed game is apt to spin the cube around like a top in a chouette.

The captain in a chouette should not stop to consult his partners about all plays. When he has an obviously automatic, or nearly automatic, play, it just wastes time to ask, "What shall I do?"

In more complicated situations the captain might move his men but leave the dice on the table to give his partners a chance to speak their minds, or in very tough situations he might even ask for suggestions.

Too much argument in a chouette is silly. You ought to speak up any time your partners are overlooking an outstanding play; but in those situations where the play suggested by the captain is just about as good as the one you like, let the captain decide.

For example, suppose 5–3 is the opening roll. You prefer moving two men from the black twelve point to your eight and ten points, but the captain wants to make the three point instead. Let him have his way without saying anything. His play is just about as good as yours; and if you argue here, he and your other partners may not listen to you when later in the game you have something really important to say.

If a player leaves the table during the progress of the game, he should ask one of his partners to act for him. If he fails to do this, he automatically goes along with the captain's moves.

Unless he has announced that he is leaving the game or that he wants to be out temporarily, he remains one of the players against the box until he returns, except of course that he cannot become captain. Thus, he moves up in line until he becomes number one, and retains that place until he gets back.

If he remains away for a long while, the other players have the right to drop him out of the game entirely, although in this instance he should take the precaution of asking to be left out temporarily after the game currently in progress is finished. In either case, when he comes back he is treated as a new entrant in the game and goes to the bottom of the line.

## Special Problems in Chouettes

For some reason, everyone seems to want to be in the box in a chouette. Theoretically, the box has the worst of it for two reasons. First, even the very best players overlook the proper move on occasion; when several players consult there is far less chance of such an oversight. Secondly, the box is always under pressure since he is playing for several times the stake of each of the other players.

Nevertheless, a winner wants the box in order to win a lot more; a loser wants the box in order to get even.

Thus, we frequently find players taking very bad doubles in an effort to hold the box or to gain the box. No opponent really objects when the box takes a bad double (since all the other players in the game stand to gain from his mistakes). But it is quite annoying to have a lone player take a double and keep everyone else out of action for a long time. Some games have a special rule to cover this, stipulating that if just one man takes a double when there is still real contact between the opposing sides, he drops to the bottom of the line if he loses the game. This won't stop the captain from taking bad doubles, but it certainly has a deterring effect on the other players.

## Buying Out a Partner

The partners in a chouette do not always see eye to eye with one another about doubling. In fact, they seldom do. When the box doubles, we have seen some players drop out, others accept doubtfully, and still others accept eagerly. We have seen times when the captain wants to double and none of his partners wants him to do so, or the absolute reverse.

The captain has the right to insist on doubling, but he seldom does so if his partners ask him to hold back. Or if he does double, he may offer to buy out any of his partners who don't want to go along. He does this by paying each of them the undoubled stake. Thus, if the captain wants to double from 2 to 4, he pays any unwilling partners two points each and takes over their games and stakes.

## Pre-empting

The box has the right to pre-empt any deals between partners. Thus, if the captain wants to buy out his four partners, the box, instead of the captain, may pay all or some of them off. This has the effect of letting the box accept the double without taking on the full liability that goes with it.

## Doubling to Get One Man Out

It is pretty good policy for the box to make a slightly unsound double (or at least one that he considers slightly unsound!) if he expects to drive one or two opponents out of the game. If his double succeeds in doing this, he has obtained an excellent result at this stage, even if the game swings against him later on.

## Settlements in Chouettes

As we will discuss in detail in the next chapter, a player may settle his game at any time. Suppose the players have doubled to 8 and their game doesn't go very well. Now a player may offer to take one point and get out. The box may counter by offering to let him out, or he may ask for one or two points.

All such offers by a player or by the box are binding until withdrawn or a roll has been made. Furthermore, an offer by a player may be accepted by any one of his partners, in which case that partner would be responsible for two games. But even after an offer has been made and accepted between partners, the box may pre-empt.

When the box offers a proposition to a specific number of players and more than that number accept, he is not bound to do business with the extra accepters. In such cases the first ones to accept his offer are accommodated.

## Drop-Takes

When the box doubles, two players may do a "drop-take." In other words, they agree to accept one double jointly and to drop the other. In the event of a drop-take, both players remain in the game, unless the chouette has a local rule to the effect that just one partner in a drop-take must play out the game by himself for the partnership.

# The Box May Take a Partner

When there are seven or more players in a game, and for some reason they don't want to make up two separate games, the box may take a partner. The partner has full rights of consultation, and he shares equally in the profits and losses. When the box and partner double, each opponent may drop out or not as he chooses; when the box is doubled the partner may drop out, but in that case the box collects the points his partner pays out and then must play on for the full doubled stake. Similarly, if the box drops out and the partner accepts a double, the partner collects from the box and plays for the full doubled stake.

We suggest the following rules for the special problems created by this game:

1. Any player except the captain may become the box's partner.
2. A player may refuse the box's invitation to become a partner.
3. The partner loses his place in line; when the box loses, the partner takes next to last place and the box last place.
4. The box is not required to take a partner.

# A Great Settlement Story

The following incident happened in a seven-handed game in Lucaya, in the Bahamas. Porter Ijams (one of the best backgammon players in the world) was one of six against the box. They had doubled to 8, and at one stage of the game Porter sold his game to one of his partners for six points. This left him out of that game with six points in the bank. The box was playing for forty-eight points (eight points times six players); a couple of plays later, Porter agreed to take a half interest in the box for six more points. This left him twelve ahead, and playing for twenty-four.

A little while later, Porter and his new partner (now the box) redoubled to 16. Three players dropped out and three accepted, whereupon the box asked Porter if he would take the twenty-four points paid by the refusers and let the box play on against the three who had accepted the double to 16. Porter agreed, and chalked up a total of thirty-six points to his credit in the ledger. To prove what a genius he was—the box finally lost the game!

The official laws for chouette are given in Chapter 15.

# 13

## SETTLEMENTS

There is no rule that requires a backgammon game to be completed. The players may settle a game any time an agreement can be reached. Sometimes veteran players will call a game off entirely after the first couple of rolls because it looks as if it will be a long game and neither player has any advantage worth capitalizing on. Or suppose the game starts with each player rolling 6–5 twice. Each man his brought his two back men to safety, and the man whose roll it is has a very slight advantage. He proceeds to dissipate this by rolling 3–1. This leaves him 4 points ahead, but it is the other player's roll. Since the average roll is 8 1/6, the game is a tossup, and will depend entirely on who rolls the better dice. There will be no excitement or chance to use skill—so, unless the players start rolling the doubling cube over and over, they might as well just set up a new game.

A more frequent opportunity for settlement occurs when the game has been doubled several times and finally depends on the result of one roll. As an example, suppose the cube is at 8, and you have one man left on your three point and one man on your five point, while your opponent has two men left on his one point. It is your roll; to win the game you must bear off both men.

If you count up, you'll find that you have fourteen possible winning and twenty-two possible losing rolls, and thus have somewhat the worst of the game. Your opponent now says, "I'll take two points," meaning he'll settle for two points instead of playing it out and possibly winning eight points.

It looks like a generous offer, but it isn't anything of the kind. As a matter of fact, in almost all instances the correct settlement turns out to be mathematically less than you would expect.

Let's work this out. Suppose you reached this position thirty-six times and played each game out. You would expect to win fourteen games and lose twenty-two for a net loss of eight games. Since the cube is at 8, your total expected loss in those thirty-six games would be eight times eight or sixty-four points, *an average of one and seven-ninths points per game.*

Thus, in this game a two-unit settlement is a trifle too much, and a one-and-one-half-unit settlement is a trifle too little.

When we settle games of this sort, we round off to a figure in dollars and cents rather than get involved in fractions of a point. In rounding off, we let the man who is ahead on the ledger take the worst of the settlement. Suppose that you were playing this game for a dollar a point. If you were ahead overall, you should pay two dollars; if you were behind, you should pay only a dollar and a half.

You may not want to get involved with settling games at all. In fact, *we recommend that you leave settlements entirely alone unless you can be sure that you know exactly what you are doing.*

Here is another example. The cube is at 32 on your side of the table. It is your opponent's roll and his last two men are on the four and one points, while you have one man on your one point. He has twenty-nine winning rolls and seven losing rolls (*check Table 4, or note that he loses if he rolls 3–2, 3–1, 2–1, or double 1*).

Thus, your net loss in thirty-six games will be twenty-two points. Since the cube is at 32, you multiply twenty-two by thirty-two to see how you would stand at the end of thirty-six games; this comes to 704 points. You now divide that total point loss of 704 by the total games involved, which is of course thirty-six. This will give you your expected loss per game, which comes to nineteen and five-ninths units.

If you were to offer to pay nineteen units in this position, the chances are that your opponent would refuse indignantly—not because the correct settlement would be a trifle more, but rather because he would feel that he was entitled to something like twenty-four to twenty-five units. In other words, he might also refuse a generous offer of twenty or twenty-one units.

Reverse the position, so that you become the man about to roll with that nineteen-and-five-ninths advantage. You might offer to take eighteen, seventeen, or even sixteen units, and your opponent would know that you were more than fair. If he did refuse your kind offer, it would probably be accompanied by some remark like "Shoot! I might as well be broke as the way I am."

We saw an example of this recently. Black had doubled to 8 in a running game, and white had rolled very well and reached a position in which two men were left on his two point while black had two men left on his one point. It was white's roll.

White was in a redoubling position. In fact, his position was so good that black barely had the proper basis for acceptance. The odds in white's favor were twenty-six to ten, or just under three to one, and the correct settlement would have been seven and one-ninth units (twenty-six less ten, or sixteen times sixteen—the number of points the cube would be at—which comes to 256, divided by the number of games, thirty-six, equals seven and one-ninth).

White was fully aware of this, but he was well ahead on the score sheet and generously offered to take just six. Black had also figured out the proper settlement and knew that white's offer was generous; nevertheless he replied, "I'd rather gamble the game out. Go ahead and redouble."

White redoubled. Then he rolled 5–2 and collected the full sixteen units.

Other apparently simple one-roll situations may have complications. As an example, look at Position 93.

It is white's roll, and he has a shot at the blot that black has been forced to leave on his five point. The odds against a hit are twenty-five to eleven, which means that in thirty-six games white would expect a net loss of fourteen.

White has some slight chance to miss this blot and still win. He may stay off the board entirely this time and perhaps several more times, only to hit this or some other blot when he finally does come in. And he has a very slight chance to win in a running game: a roll of double 6 will put him almost even; so will coming in on any 6 if they

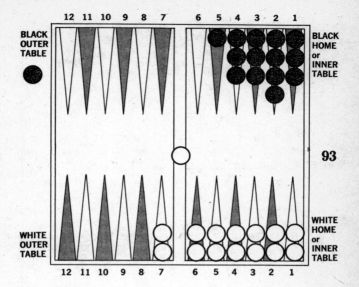

are followed by several big doubles. White also has some chance to lose a gammon. Roughly speaking, the gammon chance balanced against the other winning chances offset one another, and the proper settlement should be based on this one shot.

Assume the cube is at 4. In thirty-six games, white would expect to lose four times fourteen, or fifty-six points, an average loss of one and five-ninths points. At a dollar a point, a fair settlement would thus be a dollar and a half!

Change the black position a trifle by eliminating the man on the five point and two of the three men on the four point, leaving black's blot on his four point instead.

Now the chance that white can win a running game has practically disappeared, and the chance that he will lose a gammon has considerably increased.

He will still win if he hits that blot, but the fair settlement at this point must take the gammon chance into consideration, so white should pay two dollars or even two dollars and a half to get out of his troubles.

Change the position again by moving the two white men back from the white one point to black's outer board, Position 94. White will still win if he hits black's blot on his four point. He will almost surely be gammoned if he misses. His plus side is 11/36 times four (where the cube is at), or 44/36. His minus side is 25/36 times eight (the gammon certainty doubles the stake) or 200/36 and his net minus expectation is thus 156/36 or 4.33. Since there is some chance to miss hitting black's blot and still avoid getting gammoned, a fair settlement is probably four units.

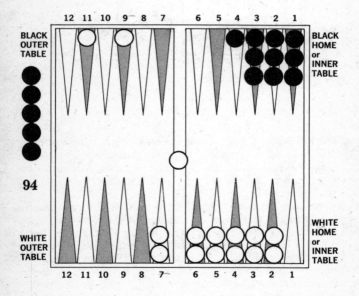

Position 95 arose in a five-handed chouette. White was in the box and at one stage had redoubled to 16. Later on the captain wanted to double to 32. His three partners all

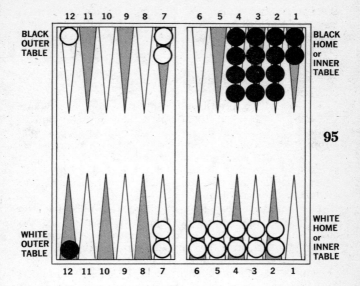

objected, and, while the captain could have doubled without his partners' consent, he offered to buy them out. They all sold their games to him at sixteen points each, and he doubled to 32. White took the double, and the game was actually for 128 since black represented four players. When Position 95 was reached, white doubled to 64 (representing a total now of 256), and black took the double.

The take was correct. Actually, white should not have doubled, since he was only a two-to-one favorite to hit black's man on the white twelve point. After the double, failure to hit black would cost him the game, since black would then control the cube and white could not afford to accept black's double to 128; while if he had not doubled, he might miss and still win. Anyway, white did double, and so they were now playing for a total of 256 units. At this point, the other players insisted that there be a settlement. Mathematically, white was entitled to one-third of

256, or eighty-five and one-third points. Black refused to pay that much, pointing out that he might still win even if white hit his blot. Finally, white accepted a very fair settlement of eighty.

## Midgame Settlements

You don't have to settle an entire game. Sometimes when the cube has reached 16 or 32 the players may want to settle or perhaps call off part of a game. As an example, suppose that you have doubled to 32 in a complicated position, and then even more complications develop. You foresee all sorts of excitement ahead, including the possibility of a double to 64 being hurled at you. You offer to withdraw your last double.

This will have the effect of putting the cube back on your side of the table. Your opponent refuses this, but makes a counterposition to let you turn the cube back to 16 provided it stays on his side of the table. This, of course, is a better proposition for him.

You now make a third proposal. Perhaps you suggest that the cube be turned to 16 and placed in the middle, so that either of you will have the right to double next. Or you might propose allowing the cube to stay on his side, provided that he will agree not to double for some specified number of rolls.

We have seen discussions of this sort go on for quite a while—and occasionally one player has said, "Let's call the whole game off," and had his offer accepted.

## Increasing the Stake

It is possible to turn the cube up by agreement. A typical situation would be when a player is obviously thinking of doubling. His opponent says, "If you double, I'll take it."

The first player now says, "How about moving the cube to 2 and leaving it where it is?"—i.e., leaving it in the center of the board, and either player may double again later.

If his opponent accepts, it is the same as an automatic double.

# Beavers

Some backgammon players like to play that when a man doubles, his opponent has the right to "beaver," or have the cube turned one extra notch. Beavers have no real part in backgammon, but they give desperate gamblers a chance to turn the cube over faster than otherwise.

# 14

# HOW TO RUN A BACKGAMMON
# TOURNAMENT

Backgammon, like most games and sports, is easily adapted to tournament play. As a matter of fact, backgammon is so versatile a game that it is adaptable to a number of different kinds of tournaments. The first step in running a tournament is to get together a group who want to play in one; the next step is to establish tournament rules and conditions of play.

Of course you will follow the regular laws of backgammon whenever possible, but you'll certainly want to eliminate automatic doubles entirely, and possibly restrict doubles and redoubles. If your tournament is run on a match-play basis, in which a match is either won or lost and the size of the victory is of no importance, there is no need to restrict regular doubling. If a man wants to lose an eight-, sixteen-, or thirty-two-point game, that is his privilege. In round-robin or other events where actual scores are counted, you should usually allow only one double and one redouble. In some cases you may also want to limit the plus score a player may win in one match, without limiting the minus score of his opponent.

Round-robin tournaments are most suitable for one-session and club events, or for a group of people at home. Any number can play. Thus, if you have twenty players together for an afternoon or evening, you might divide them into two groups of ten each and have each player in group A play three-game matches against each of six players in group B. After each match, the players in group A remain seated and the players in group B move forward one player, until six matches have been played. Then, as a finale, the player with the best score in group A could play a longer match (i.e., more than three games) against the player in group B with the best score; the winner wins the championship.

Another type of round-robin event is used by the Metro-politan Inter-Club League of New York. Some ten clubs get together twice a year; each club has a five-member team, and each man plays against one man from every other club. Automatic doubles are barred, and regular doubles are limited to one double and one redouble, but full plus and minus scores are kept. The winning team is the one with the highest total plus score. More on round-robin tournaments later.

## Elimination Matches

The standard procedure in other tournaments is a tennis-type series of elimination matches, with the matches get-ting longer (i.e., more points are needed to win) as the finals are approached. Elimination tournaments are best run for groups of 16, 32, 64, 96, 128, 192, or 256 players (though it's usually preferable to have a few less than these numbers, giving several players "bye"). Tennis-type scoring is also used, except that there are no deuce matches. Thus, in an eleven-point match the first player to reach a total of eleven wins, even though his opponent may have scored ten points.

To make the selection of players impersonal, each player is usually numbered and the numbers put into a hat and pulled out to see who plays whom. After playing the first round, winners go through the same process to pick their opponents in the second round, and so on, each round reducing the number of players by half until the finals produce the winner. Depending on how much time you have for the tournament, the number of points each round is played for is usually increased after the first round.

Since (at tournaments, at least) the average backgam-mon game usually takes from six to eight minutes, the number of points a match is played for varies according to the number of players in relation to the time available for the tournament. Thus, if you have only one afternoon or evening and there are sixteen players, the first match might be played for seven points (i.e., the first man to win at least seven points takes the match). With sixty-four players, two additional rounds of matches are played, so the first round might be played for five points. Large tournaments that go on for four or five days usually start the first round at thirteen or fifteen points; each round thereafter increases by two points.

The higher the number of points you're playing a match for, the more skill you need to win; the lower the number of points, the more that lucky rolls of the dice will help you win.

The typical tournament held in an afternoon or evening might have sixty-four players. It will usually take three to four hours if the first round is played for five points, and the semifinals and finals are played for seven or possibly nine points. Usually these events begin at two o'clock in the afternoon or nine in the evening; players who don't show up after a ten-minute grace period are defaulted. Often a time limit is set for each round; the rules committee might stipulate that no match can last longer than forty-five minutes. If two players are still tied, the player rolling high dice might become the winner; or if the score indicates that the current game could produce a tournament winner, the rules committee might allow the game to continue to its end.

It is always best to have a general list of tournament rules available to all players at the registration desk. Here is a list of widely used rules:

1. All entries are subject to approval by the tournament (rules) committee.

2. Players should move their men with only one hand.

3. Players should begin each round punctually and play at a "comfortable" pace.

4. The tournament committee may impose a time limit on any round.

5. Players should play in relative silence.

6. Judges may be assigned to any round; all rounds in the Championship Flight will be assigned judges from quarterfinals on up. Any player may request that a judge supervise any round.

7. At the start of any game either player may ask to mix the dice. In this case he shakes the four dice together in

one cup and rolls them out. The opponent selects a die—then the roller—then the opponent—with the roller then taking the last one.

8. If any difference of opinion develops, all men will be left frozen on the board until a judge is sent for. He, with at least one member of the tournament committee, will make the necessary ruling, and their decision will be final. But no play can be contested once the next throw of the dice has been made.

9. Both dice must be thrown again if either die is not rolled out flat on the board; if a die lands flat on a man, it is still considered cocked and both dice must be rethrown. A player may not offer a double before recasting, however, since play is considered to have started once the dice are thrown, cocked or not.

10. If a player throws his dice prematurely, before his opponent has finished his move, the dice must be rethrown.

11. Both players should keep score, unless they agree in advance that only one of them need do so.

12. Spectators are expected to be silent during play, and any spectator may be barred from watching a match.

Before the tournament, the chairman should meet with the tournament committee to decide on how to interpret the rules, so that each ruling can be given quickly and decisively.

Prize money, if any, should be distributed according to the number of players and the type of tournament. It is gathered either by paying part of the entry fees into a pool, by special contributions from the players, by an auction pool of some sort, or by a combination of the three. With sixteen players there should be four prizes, with thirty-two there should be six; with sixty-four at least eight, and so on.

In elimination events it is advisable to have a "consolation," so that first-round losers will have something to do.

At large tournaments the most common seating arrangement is to set up rows of long tables. On each table backgammon boards are placed about a foot apart. Ashtrays, a scorepad, and a pencil are provided each player. At one end of the room, near the middle so that everyone can read it, is the scoreboard. Nearby is the registration desk.

Some groups or clubs that hold weekly tournaments increase interest and attendance by giving an additional prize at the end of the year to the player winning the most rounds during the year. A small percentage of the tournament's prize money is held in reserve each week. Each player receives one point for every round won, and the player who has won the largest number of individual matches at the end of the year wins this bonus prize.

Doubling is usually allowed in elimination tournaments. Since it makes no difference what you win or lose by, you must vary your doubling and redoubling tactics with the score. Thus, if you need only one point to win the match, there is no reason for you to double under any circumstances—you can win a match only once. Conversely, if your opponent needs only one point to win, it behooves you to double at your first legal opportunity. If he accepts, you are playing for two points; he is playing for the same two points, but the extra point can do him no good.

You should also watch the gammon situation most carefully. For instance, if your opponent has doubled you to 2 and needs four points to win the match, be careful not to make a play or plays that will risk a gammon.

## International Backgammon Tournaments

In 1964 Prince Alexis Obolensky of Palm Beach conceived the idea of an international backgammon tournament to be held in the Bahamas, where gambling is perfectly legal and the weather perfectly fine. The first tournament attracted thirty-two entries, mostly from that portion of international society known as the jet set. It was won by Charles Wacker of Chicago, who beat Porter Ijams of New York in the finals. There was a fair-sized Calcutta Pool, and everyone had a good time.

In 1965 there were sixty-four entries, including a few from Europe. The winner was John Crawford, and Judd Streicher of New York was runner-up. There was the same number of players in 1966, when Oswald Jacoby won for the first time, beating runner-up Tony Vincent of Miami. Jacoby won again in 1967, when there were 128 entries, and again in 1968. Runners-up were Walter Cooke (1967) and Oakleigh Thorne (1968), both of New York. In 1969

and 1970 Walter Cooke won, and the runners-up were
Oswald Jacoby (1969) and John Geary (1970).

Obolensky also conducted similar tournaments at the
Sands Hotel in Las Vegas in 1967 and 1968. There were
approximately 128 players in each, and Tim Holland won
both the 1967 and 1968 tournaments. Porter Ijams was
runner-up in 1967 and Reginald Kernan of Paris was
runner-up in 1968.

In London the Clermont Club has run tournaments an-
nually since 1966. The first was won by Tim Holland; the
others by Charles Jardine, Greville Howard, The Honour-
able Michael Pearson, and in 1970, Claude Beer. Crock-
ford's Club also ran a tournament in 1966, and the winner
was Tobias Stone of New York. A tournament was held in
Estoril, Portugal, in 1969. It was won by Lynn Madliner
of London, and Owen Traynor of Fort Lauderdale was
runner-up.

In the 1970 Bahamas tournament the matches started
with thirteen points for the first round and increased two
points a round to a final match of twenty-five points.

The British clubs played shorter matches all the way
down the line. From the standpoint of skill, this does not
result in as good a tournament since the longer the match,
the greater the advantage to better players—but it does
get the tournament over a great deal more quickly.

## Consolation Flights

The Bahamas and Las Vegas tournaments all lasted for
four days, with two elimination matches played each of the
first three days and the finals played on the fourth day. It
was essential that something be done for the players eliminated, so there were two consolation flights and one "sympathy flight."

Here is how these events were handled in the 1970
tournament in the Bahamas: there were slightly fewer
than 128 entries, so about 90 players (i.e., those eliminated
in the two rounds held on the first day) became eligible
for the first consolation. Four matches were played the
first day of this consolation, narrowing it down to eight
players. First-round consolation matches were played for
eleven points; second-round matches for twelve; third-

round matches for thirteen; and fourth-round matches for fifteen points. Players were allowed to play a fourth-round match on the morning of the next day, but no one had to.

The last three rounds in the first consolation were seventeen, nineteen, and twenty-one points.

The second consolation was open to all players eliminated from either event by the end of the second tournament day. This meant that all but the sixteen players competing in the quarterfinals of the tournament and the first consolation were eligible.

Seven rounds were again necessary, but with only two days left to play, an effort was made to get through six rounds on the first day. The matches were played for seven, eight, nine, eleven, thirteen, and fifteen points, with the seventeen-point final round scheduled for the last day. Actually, only five rounds were completed on the first day, so there were four players left in this event on the last day of the tournament.

The sympathy flight on the last day was open to everyone except the eight players remaining in the other events. Seven rounds were played, each for five points.

In dividing the pool, prizes were given to the last eight in the tournament, the last four in each consolation, and the finalists in the sympathy flight.

## Beginners' Tournaments

There were so many novice players in attendance at these tournaments that beginners' events were held at the same time. These attracted almost as many players as the championship contest. They consisted of very short matches, and no doubling cube could be used—the theory being that a beginner could not be expected to understand how to use the cube properly. Gammons counted, of course.

There were consolation flights in the beginners' events, as well.

## How to Vary Your Play in a Tournament

As we've said, in the usual elimination match the score is all-important. If you are playing a match to thirteen points, it doesn't matter if you win thirteen to nothing, thirteen to twelve, or twenty-one to ten. You still have won your match. It also doesn't matter to the loser if his opponent winds up with a total score of fifty; he has lost only that one match.

Thus, you should use the doubling cube with great care, with one conspicuous exception, as we've mentioned before. That is when your opponent needs just one more point to win the match. In this spot you should double immediately. Don't wait until your position would warrant a double under ordinary circumstances; make your opponent play for two points right from the start.

## The Crawford Rule

At the Bahamas and Las Vegas tournaments it was felt that this doubling privilege was rather unfair. One proposed solution was to forbid doubles once a player got within one point of victory, but it was agreed that this might lead to an interminable series of dull single games in the event that one man had something like a twenty-to-ten lead in a twenty-one-point match.

John Crawford, who is always chairman of the tournament committee at these events, devised a rule providing that once a player gets within one point of victory, there can be no double in the first game after that; however, doubling would be allowed in the match from then on. This gives the player who has come so close to victory a *one*-game safety in which his opponent cannot double immediately and then happen to win a lucky gammon or backgammon to snatch away the victory.

## Playing for Gammons

In regular backgammon games you play for gammons when the position is appropriate, as a matter of course. In tournaments you should give far more thought to gammons.

At one tournament Tim Holland was leading seventeen to twelve in an nineteen-point match; we watched him play the next game for gammon right from the start. He obtained an early advantage but knew that, if he doubled, his opponent would quit the game and leave Tim one point shy of victory in the match. So Tim went ahead and took a couple of extra chances to get into gammon position. Of course he risked losing that game, but had a healthy lead and wanted to try to end the match—and he did.

We also saw Barclay Cooke refuse a double under very unusual circumstances. Barclay was leading sixteen to thirteen in a seventeen-point match. In the next game his opponent's first roll was 3–1 and he made his five point. Barclay rolled 5–4 and moved men to his eight and nine points. His opponent then made one of those "I have nothing to lose" doubles, and Barclay refused. His reasoning was that "If he follows with a couple of good rolls, he'll be able to play for a gammon. I can refuse this double and still get to play two more games; if I accept and he gammons me, he wins the match with this one."

When you're leading in a match, be very careful about offering your opponent an early double. You may not be prepared for his redouble that may come right back at you. On the other hand, when you're behind you can and should double quite freely; you'll be surprised to see how often your opponent will refuse and give you the game. There is an important exception here: don't make an unsound double when your opponent needs only two points to run the match out.

## Playing Your Opponent

At the time that Tony Vincent reached the finals of the Bahamas Tournament against Oswald Jacoby in 1967 he was a comparative newcomer to backgammon. So he felt that his best chance against Jacoby was to get the doubling cube rolling. He doubled early and often. Jacoby, on the other hand, refused to get into that trap; he wanted to keep the match from being decided quickly, on the theory that the more games it took, the better his chance to win the match.

Both were correct. If you feel that you play better than your opponent, avoid hasty doubles and don't be quick to accept them from your opponent. If you think you have the worse of the skill, take more chances and hope the doubling cube is used often. You can be lucky for a few games, but it is unlikely that your luck will hold over a long series of games against a more skilled opponent.

As an example of this theory in action, Gordon Leib refused a double in a first-round match that he would surely have accepted from any but a very poor player. The match was for thirteen points, and Gordon was trailing six to five. His opponent obviously knew little about the game, but in spite of that he had a one-point lead going into this key game. He doubled early in the game, and Gordon accepted. In the running game Gordon found himself far enough ahead so that the odds in his favor had to be at least four to one. He redoubled to 4. His opponent accepted and proceeded to roll such good dice that he became a two-to-one favorite, and redoubled to 8.

Gordon had a choice between refusing, and therefore trailing ten points to five in the match, or accepting and letting that one game decide the match. Against a player of equal ability Gordon would have accepted the double; against this player he figured that he would have a very good chance to win the match even though he was then trailing ten points to five. He refused the double. His theory was why let the fickle dice beat him in a running game when skill in all-around play would help decide the next games?

We can't tell what would have happened if Gordon had accepted—but we do know that he did pull out from that ten-to-five position and won the match. Of course, in a game for money he would have taken the double without hesitation.

## Round-Robin Play

As we've said, round-robin events are usually one-session affairs in which each contestant plays several short matches against different opponents and carries his net plus or minus score from each match.

In large round-robin tournaments each backgammon table is numbered and one side is labeled "North" and the other "South." North players remain stationary, while South players move after each match to the next higher number (players at the highest number move down to the lowest, keeping in rotation). Since there are many players and usually only three or four hours available, each player usually plays four to six matches, composed of three games each. The total number of points won is placed opposite each player's name on the scoreboard. If four matches are being played, the player with the most points accumulated at the end of the four matches wins the tournament.

It is customary at round-robin tournaments either to have no doubling or to allow just one double and one redouble. But even in a three-game match in which only one double and redouble are allowed, it is possible for the match to be won by as much as thirty-six to nothing. This would occur if, in each game, the cube reached 4 and the loser were backgammoned. There won't be many of these scores in a three-game match, but you will on occasion see sixteen-to-zero scores, and we have even seen one score of tweny-four to zero.

In order to win a round-robin tournament you have to win some of your matches by big scores. It may be very gratifying to win all your matches by scores like two to one, four to two, etc., but a net plus of twelve after six matches is not going to win the tournament for you.

Since you have only one chance in each game to double, use the cube sparingly. However, you should take chances to win a gammon or backgammon whenever possible.

As we mentioned at the beginning of the chapter, round-robin play is used by the Metropolitan Inter-Club Backgammon League in New York City, made up of ten of the most prominent clubs in the city. Each club fields a five-man team, and they get together twice a year at the Metropolitan Club to play a complete round robin. Each team numbers its players from one to five, and all number ones on each team play the number-one player on each of the other nine clubs, all number twos play each of the other nine number twos, and so on down the line. Thus, if all ten of the clubs compete, nine matches of three games each, or twenty-seven games, completes the event. In each game one double and one redouble are allowed.

At the end, the winning club is the team whose total score of its five players is the greatest.

Another type of round-robin tournament is what might be called an "individual" round robin. In this kind each participant plays every other player a match consisting of a specified number of points, often over several days. Doubling is allowed, but the scoring is a little different. No matter how high a score he may win the match by, the winner of each match is simply credited with a plus one, the loser with a zero. This serves a very important purpose: if you win a lucky match by a large number of points, you do not suddenly take a big lead in the entire field; instead you simply are credited with one winning match.

Let's take an example where you have fifteen players. If you have several days in which to run your tournament, you might play fourteen matches consisting of eleven points each (remember that an eleven-point match means that the first player to reach eleven points is the winner—not that one player must win by a margin of eleven points). If you have just one evening for the tournament, you would play no more than a three-point match. If you're playing a beginners' round robin, we suggest that each match consist of just one game, in which case you would not use the doubling cube at all.

At the end of the fourteen games in your fifteen-player individual round robin, the player with the most winning points is the champion. Remember that winning a match gives you only one point, so if the fifteen players are evenly matched, ten points is probably sufficient to win.

If there is a tie for first place after all matches are concluded, the final champion is determined by the result of the match that the two winners previously played against each other.

## Duplicate Tournaments

The duplicate variation of round-robin tournaments is particularly suited for less-experienced players. There should be fourteen or sixteen players at most, since with more players it would probably take too long to finish.

Let's say there are sixteen players. Eight backgammon tables are set up, each table numbered and labeled North and South. At one end of the room one person rolls the dice and calls out the numbers rolled in turn for North and South until all games are finished.

The great fun in this game is noting the diverse results. Sometimes the games will be identical for two, three, or even four moves, but by the sixth move the chances are that all positions will be radically different. As the game develops, you may even have gammons on both sides of the table!

When all games are finished, each South player moves up one table, as in a round-robin tournament.

Usually there is a limit of one double and one redouble per game.

# 15

# THE OFFICIAL LAWS OF BACKGAMMON

As we said in the Introduction, back in 1931 Wheaton Vaughan, the chairman of the Card and Backgammon Committee of the Racquet and Tennis Club of New York, invited representatives of other clubs to join with the Racquet Club in order to produce a code of laws for backgammon. That code was soon universally adopted and accepted generally. As far as we know, Oswald Jacoby is the only member of the committee still alive, but their laws have lasted with practically no change, and the laws presented here are essentially the same. They have been prepared in conjunction with the International Backgammon Association and the Inter-Club League of New York.

Remember that laws are made to prevent arguments, not to cause them. Never attempt to use the laws to gain an advantage.

## The Game

1. The game of backgammon is played by two persons.
2. Thirty men—fifteen of one color and fifteen of another—are used, and are set up as shown on page 200, on a standard board of four quarters or tables having six points each.

In diagram 96 the players' home boards (or inner tables) are shown at the right. This means that white's home board is opposite his right hand, and black's home board opposite his left hand. In actual play it is customary to have the home boards nearer the light.

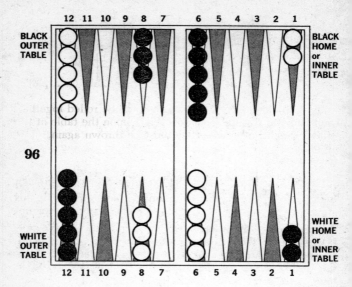

3. For entering and bearing off, the points in both inner tables are considered as numbered from one to six, beginning with the point nearest the edge of the board.

4. Direction of play is from adversary's inner table to adversary's outer table, to player's outer table, and then to player's inner (home) table.

5. Play of the men is governed by two dice, thrown (cast) from a cup in which the dice are shaken before casting.

6.(a) For the first game either player may ask to roll for choice of seats, men, or dice. Otherwise they just sit down, set the men up, and play.

6.(b) At the start of any later game either player may ask to mix the dice. In this case he shakes the four dice together in one cup and rolls them out. The opponent selects a die—then the roller—then the opponent—with the roller then taking the last one.

# The Throws

7. For the opening throw, each player throws a single die. Every tie requires another opening throw. Whoever throws the higher number wins, and for his first move plays the numbers upon both dice. After that each player in turn throws two dice.

8. The dice must be shaken thoroughly, rolled together, and come to rest flat (not "cocked") upon the table at the player's right, otherwise they must be thrown again.

9. There must be a rethrow if a throw is made before an adversary's play is completed.

10. A play is deemed completed when a player moves his men and starts to pick up his dice. If he has picked them up before playing all numbers he legally can, his opponent has the right to compel him to complete or not to complete his play. A roll by the opponent is an acceptance of the play as made (see Law 19).

# The Play

11. The play of the men consists of:

(a) Moving a man (or men) the exact number of points indicated by the number on each of the two dice thrown. One man may be moved the total of the two dice thrown, or one man may be moved the number shown on one die, and an entirely different man the number shown on the other die.

(b) Entering a man, in the adversary's inner table, on a point corresponding to the number on a die thrown.

(c) Bearing off a man in the player's inner table, when no man is left outside that table or on the bar, in accordance with Law 17.

12. Doublets require four plays of the number on the dice.

13. Plays must be made for both dice if possible. Either number may be played first. If either number may be played, but not both, then the higher number thrown must be played.

14. No play may be made which lands, or touches down, on a point held by two or more of the adversary's men.

15. When a play lands on a point occupied by a single man (blot) of the adversary's, such a man is "hit" and must be lifted from the board by the hitter and placed on the bar in the center of the playing board, to await entry in accordance with Law 11b.

16. A player having a man on the bar may not play any other man until that man has been entered.

17. When in a position to bear off, you may bear off a man from a point corresponding to the number on a die thrown, or from the highest occupied point which is lower than the number indicated by a die. If a number is thrown for an unoccupied point, no man below can be borne off, using such number, while any man remains on a higher point. You are not required to bear off a man if you are able to move a man forward on the board. Law 13 applies here as in all other situations.

For example, in Diagram 97 you roll 6–1. You may use the 1 to move from your six point to your five point, and then use the 6 to bear a man from the five point; thus, you don't leave a man exposed to a hit by black's men on your one point. In other words, Law 13, stating that *as long as you play both numbers you may play either one first,* applies in bearing off as well as at all other times.

## Errors

18. If an error has been made in the setup, it must be corrected if either player notices it before the second play of the game has been completed.

19. If an error in play has been made, either player may require its correction before a subsequent throw. The man played in error must be correctly played; however, the player may replay his entire move.

## Scoring

20. A game is won by the player who first bears off all of his men.

A gammon (double game) is won if the adversary has not borne off a single man. This doubles the count.

A backgammon (triple game) is won if the adversary

212

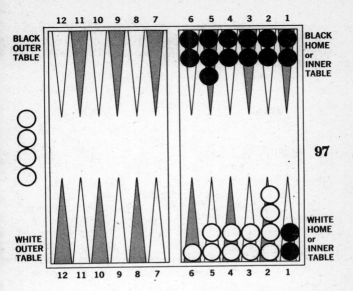

has not borne off a single man and has one or more men in the winner's inner table or upon the bar. This triples the count.

21. Doubling game. The count is raised:

(a) *Automatically:* Each tie in the opening throw doubles the previous count. Automatic doubles are not played unless the players have agreed to use them and an understanding has been reached as to the method and limitation of such doubles.

(b) *Voluntarily:* Either player may offer the first optional double of the previous count. After that the right to double the previous count alternates, being always with the player who accepted the last double.

A double or redouble may be offered only when it is the player's turn to play and before he has thrown the dice. He shall be deemed to have thrown the dice even if he rolls cocked dice.

A double may be accepted or declined. The refusal of a double terminates the game, and the player refusing loses whatever the count may amount to before the double was offered.

22. Gammons double or triple the last count.

## Chouette *

23. Chouette is played by three or more members.

24. In beginning the game each member shall throw a die. The one throwing the highest number is then the "man in the box," the next highest is the "captain." The other members, in accordance with each one's throw, rank below the captain and succeed him in that order.

25. The initial throw shall determine each member's position, but in the event of a tie only those tying throw again for their position. The highest or higher number always has precedence.

26. Any applicant to a chouette may be accepted. He becomes the last ranking member in the first game in which he participates.

27. After the positions have been determined, the man in the box and the captain proceed as in the two-handed game except that all the remaining members are partners of the captain.

28. The man in the box plays alone and scores separately against each one of his adversaries. He retains his position until defeated. In such event, he retires as a player and takes his place as last ranking member (unless there be an added member). The previous captain then becomes the man in the box.

29. The captain may consult with any or all of the partners on any question that may arise in the course of the game. He is, however, the final arbiter, except as hereafter provided. Should he be defeated, he loses his position and takes his place as last ranking member (unless

---

* In a chouette too much discussion and contention slows up the game. The captain should ask for advice only when he is really in doubt as to the play, and partners should give advice only when they think the captain is overlooking a play entirely or when they want to suggest that he double.

214

there be an added member). The highest ranking partner then becomes captain.

30. All partners are bound by the action of the captain except in the case of a double by the man in the box. In this case any player has the right to refuse or accept the double, irrespective of the action by the captain.

31. Should the captain decline to accept a double offered by the man in the box, he loses his position and forfeits to the man in the box his count previous to the proposed double.

32. When a double has been declined by the captain, any or all of the other members may accept it. The highest ranking of those accepting becomes captain until the termination of that game.

33. Accepting or declining a double does not change the rank of any member when the new captain loses; if the new captain wins, he takes the box.

34. Those players who refuse to accept the double are out of that game and may not consult from then on.

# 16

# POSTSCRIPT TO THE LAWS: VARIATIONS OF PLAY

Master the laws given in the previous chapter thoroughly. The laws should be followed explicitly in tournaments, but in your own play you may want to make certain modifications. This chapter discusses some widely used modifications in the laws, and then several other potential variations in "house rules." As long as a variation does not materially change the character of the game, we see no reason why you shouldn't go along with the crowd. However, it is important that you fully understand the effect that each variation has on the game.

First, three fairly common modifications in the laws:

## Modification 1: No Backgammons

The play to win a gammon involves considerable skill, and gammons should be an important feature of the game. But winning a backgammon is usually the result of extraordinarily good luck on the winner's part and bad luck on the loser's part. You appreciate winning a triple game, but your victim is mighty annoyed, so many people just don't like to count triple games.

In fact, in Britain and Europe triple games aren't counted at all. If you want to make it a rule in your own games not to count triples, that is up to you, though we prefer the normal play. Just make sure that you make it clear in advance, and everyone agrees.

# Modification 2: No Gammons in Undoubled Games

This is sometimes called the Jacoby rule since Oswald Jacoby first suggested it. His contention is that a player will occasionally gain an overwhelming superiority at a very early stage and decide to play on for gammon, rather than double and end the game right there, winning only the lower stake. In tournaments he will of course play to win the gammon. And in individual games, if the game has already been doubled, there is no reason why he should not be allowed to go after the extra points. But when there has been no double at all, it is likely to be a long, boring game (particularly to the loser) with the doubling cube never in use. Thus, some players adopt the Jacoby rule—no gammon allowed in an undoubled game—which allows the opponent to concede a single game and get a new game started. This does speed up the game, and since it is fair to both players we use it ourselves whenever possible.

Some people play the Jacoby rule as long as there has been no *regular* double (as opposed to automatic doubles); we prefer to play it only when the cube is at 1.

The Jacoby rule tends to change the play of single games. Each player can afford to take very wild chances in the early game since until there is a double he can always get out with the loss of just one point. Furthermore, the man who gains an early advantage says to himself, "If I don't double now, the best I can do is to win one point. If I double and my opponent refuses, I get that one point immediately. If he accepts, I can win two, four, or six points, depending on whether I can gammon or back-gammon him."

# Modification 3: Suggestions for Chouettes

A player in a chouette can consult with the captain but must defer to him except when a double or redouble is involved. If the box doubles, a player may accept or decline regardless of what the captain does—but if the captain insists on doubling, his partners have no say. It is the captain's decision that holds.

We feel that the following rule for a chouette is far preferable:

(a) When the captain insists on doubling and *a majority of his partners* object, they may demand that the captain pay them off at the current game stake. In this case the man in the box has the right to pre-empt and pay them off.

(b) When the captain insists on doubling and *half or less of his partners* object, the objectors may withdraw from the game entirely. In this case the man in the box has the right to demand that the captain take over their games.

The man in the box frequently pre-empts under (a) to reduce his liability. We have never seen him pre-empt under (b).

As an example, assume the captain has two partners. The game is at 4 and the captain insists on doubling to 8. Both partners object, whereupon the captain pays them each four points and proceeds to double to 8. If the box accepts, each side is playing for a total of twenty-four units, but the captain who insisted on doubling has already paid out eight units to his erstwhile partners.

This rule has one very salutary effect: it stops annoyance doubles and redoubles by captains.

Here are some other variations of the game that you should be familiar with:

## Extra Starting Doubles (Optional Rerolls)

In the simplest form of this variation, each player rolls one die (which in itself might produce an automatic double), and if the high man does not like his opening roll, he turns the doubling cube one notch higher and rolls both his dice. He must then play the new roll.

In most games where this option is allowed, the second player is also allowed to try a second roll if he doesn't like his first one, provided that he turns the cube before he takes that second roll.

It is usually provided also that if either player's roll is a doublet, the cube is automatically turned once more for that.

Even this rather simple little variation is likely to start

the cube rolling over and over. Suppose that each player rolls an opening 4. The cube automatically goes to 2. Next they roll 5 and 1. The higher player turns the cube to 4 and proceeds to roll double 5. He has to take this as his opening move, but the cube now goes to 8 since he rolled a doublet. And the second player hasn't gotten around to doing anything yet. He proceeds to roll double 6, another automatic double. Naturally he accepts his roll and plays it, but the cube is now at 16 and the game has only just started!

To prevent the cube from going too high in this type of optional reroll game, it is usually agreed beforehand to play a minimum of 2 and a maximum of 8 on the cube. Even if the cube reaches 8 before the second player rolls, he is still entitled to a second roll if he doesn't like his first.

## Initial Double Dice

In this game each player starts by rolling *both* his dice. High man (doublets count as plain totals only—thus double 4 would count 8, etc.) gets the first roll, and he has the option of turning the cube and rolling again. His opponent also gets the right to a second roll if he doesn't like what comes up the first time.

Let's see how the opening doubles mount up here. If the players roll the same total (say one rolls double 4 and the other 3–5), the tie produces an automatic double and there must be a reroll. If both roll identical numbers such as 5–4, this counts as *two* automatic doubles. And any time a doublet is rolled there is also an automatic double!

## Limitation of Doubles

If you ever run into anyone who wants to play either of these games with no limitation on the number of opening doubles, we have a simple recommendation: don't play! You can't afford it, and neither, probably, can he.

In places such as New York's Racquet Club where double dice used to be played frequently, a limitation is placed on the cube: the game must start at either 4 or

8. In other words, players simply play for four times the agreed stake, with one automatic double possible.

It is easy to estimate the effect of this game. If the stake is one dollar a point, you are playing for either four or eight dollars. Actually, you should assume that you are playing for eight, because most of the time you will get to the upper limit.

Similarly, if you play with a minimum of 2 and a maximum of 8, bear in mind that you will seldom start at 2 and most of the time you'll be at 8.

We are pleased to report that these multiple double games seem to be dying out. They remind us of the very wealthy Texan who was about to play in a new gin rummy game. The players started talking about six games across; spades double; hearts triple; and diamonds four times; with extra boxes for gins, undercuts, and special hands. The Texan listened awhile and then said, "I'm a country boy. Let's play just one game of straight gin, but since you want to gamble, how about ten dollars a point?"

The same principle applies here: if you want to gamble, play for high stakes—but play a sensible game.

## Technique of Double-Dice Play

If you're playing with initial double dice, when you get a good first roll such as 3–1, 4–2, or 6–1, keep it. If you do reroll and your second roll is a poor one, tend to play safely. Thus, if your second roll is 5–3, just automatically make your three point. Don't bring two men down from your opponent's twelve point, exposing a man on your ten point. Remember that your opponent will get two shots at it, since he too will have the option of rolling again if he doesn't like his first roll.

The second player should vary his play even more. Suppose that you are playing that the game must start at either 4 or 8. Your opponent has started with double aces, and the cube is at 4. You proceed to roll a poor number. Play it anyway! Why move the cube to 8 (which you have to do in order to reroll), when you already have much the worst of the game?

A word to the wise here: lots of double-dice players automatically take their second roll in order to get the

220

game up. Don't do this. If you have a good first roll, take it; your reroll might be a horror.

## Duplicate Backgammon

In this form of backgammon, several games are played with the same rolls. Although this fascinating game can be played by an even number of players, the most usual game is four players. The match is played two against two. The players at one table throw the dice. As each player makes his roll he calls out his number for the member of his team to play at the other table. Care must be taken not to call out the present throw until the other table is ready, as the thrower's partner at the next table might not have completed his last play.

The score is kept by simply putting the scores together at both tables. If player A at table one lost two, and his opposite number at table two won four, then team A is plus two at the end of the first game.

Even with the most expert players it is remarkable to see how quickly the various positions become different from one another at the two or more tables that are in play.

Duplicate backgammon is becoming extremely popular in clubs in New York, and starting to spread around the country in much the same way as duplicate bridge did forty years ago.

# 17

# OTHER FORMS OF BACKGAMMON

As we noted in the Introduction, in some ancient forms of the game three dice were used, and boards of varying design. But in all the forms of backgammon that are played today around the world, two dice are used and each player moves fifteen men around the standard backgammon board. In all forms the object is to bring them into the home board and then bear them off.

However, in some forms of the game there are no blots at all; one man may control the point he is on instead of two, and six single men in a row then form a prime.

Doubles are usually played four times, but in a few versions doubles warrant extra plays. And though usually if a man can't play his whole roll he loses the rest of his moves, in some forms of the game his opponent can then play the unused moves.

In several versions the men are not arranged around the board at the start of the game; either they all begin off the board or all on one point.

We couldn't possibly cover all the forms of the game played today, but we can discuss, briefly, a few of the more interesting ones. We'll begin with a couple of beginners' games.

## Eureika

In the Middle East children are taught to play backgammon by first learning this simple game. Each player puts three men each on his one, two, and three points, and two men each on his four, five, and six points. As usual, to begin, each player throws one die, and whoever throws the higher roll plays first. After a player rolls his dice, he takes off a man on each point corresponding to the number thrown. The first to bear off all fifteen men wins the game.

There is only an infinitesimal amount of skill involved, and the man who gets first play is usually the winner.

## Blast-off

This simple game is our own invention. The setup is the same as for backgammon except that each player's two back men (formerly on the opponent's one point) have been brought forward to join the five men on the opponent's twelve point. Play proceeds as in regular backgammon, but no blots can ever be hit; it is just a question of which player rolls the higher dice.

There is a little skill involved in learning how to use your rolls to best advantage. Moreover, if played with the doubling cube you can learn when to double or not to double in running games. In other words, beginners can have some fun and learn something.

## Moultezim

In addition to regular backgammon, Turks play a variation called *moultezim*, quite different in character, beginning with the board and setup of men. In moultezim white's one point (and inner board) is at the lower right, as in regular backgammon, but black's one point (and inner board) is at the upper *left* instead of the upper right; black's twelve point (and outer board) is at the upper *right*, where his one point and inner board are in regular backgammon. In the setup, all fifteen of white's men start on black's twelve point (the old black one point) and black's fifteen men start on white's twelve point (also the white twelve point in the regular game). Black must move all of his men the full twenty-four points around the board: first to the right from white's twelve point in the white outer board, into white's inner board, then into the black outer board (his inner board in the conventional game, remember), then to his own (new) inner board, and off to the left (instead of the right as in regular backgammon). White also moves in a counterclockwise direction: from the black twelve point in black's outer board into the black inner board, then into the white outer board and into the white inner board and off to the right, the same as in the regular game.

The primary strategy is to create a prime, in order to block your opponent's progress into his home board; following that, you run and bear off your men.

The rules of play are the same as for backgammon except that:

1. Men are not hit or sent home; there are no blots. A single man controls the point he is on in the same way as two men control it in backgammon, and his opponent then cannot stop on that point.

2. You are not allowed to occupy more than four points in your outer board. This means that you are not allowed to establish a prime right in front of your opponent's starting point on your twelve point.

3. To begin the game, each player rolls one die. The high man then rolls both dice for his first play.

4. You must move one man into your own outer or inner board before you can move a second man from the starting point. In other words, you must get your first man past your opponent's men on your twelve point before moving any others.

This fourth rule may not seem important, but just see what happens to you if your first four rolls should happen to be double 6, double 6, double 3, and double 1. Since black occupies your twelve point, you can move only one 6 with the first roll, and you can't move at all on the second roll. On your third turn to play you can move that forward man three more spaces, and on your fourth turn you can play two of the four aces. By this time your opponent will have moved one man across the dividing line past your other men piled up, and he will have placed a couple of other men in your outer board; suppose that they occupy your nine and ten points. Now you roll 4–1 and once more can't play. Two plays later he will have completed a prime in your outer board against that man of yours, and you won't be able to play at all until he breaks his prime.

Now he will proceed to move his other nine men around

the board, and barring accidents he will use six of them to form a second prime stretching from his ten point to his five point (remember that he must leave the eleven point open: Rule 2). Then he will break his prime in your outer board, and at last after you have been able to move that one man into your own board, you will be able to move one of your other fourteen men still on his twelve point—but only if you roll an ace.

Of course, most of the time in moultezim each player will get his first man around into his outer board in two or three turns and will then be able to move other men. At this stage of play you should try to occupy one or two more points in your outer board and as many points as possible in your opponent's outer board (right in front of your starting point). It is almost always very poor tactics to move any of your men into your inner board in the early play.

If you can establish a prime anywhere in your own board, you should win the game. Establishing a prime in your opponent's board is by no means as valuable, since his men blocked by your prime will be far closer to home than your men in your prime will be, thus giving you little advantage in the running game once you break the prime.

Even if you can't make a prime, remember that each point you occupy in either board belongs to you, and the advantage in moultezim—as in all forms of backgammon—goes to the man who holds the greater number of points.

## Acey-deucy

This game is played in the American Navy. It is close enough to some Mediterranean variations of backgammon to suggest that it was picked up there.

In this game all the men start off the board. They enter and move around the board in the same way as men sent home in regular backgammon. In other words, the white men enter in black's home board and move around through black's outer board and white's outer board until all are gathered in white's home board; then white can start to bear them off. Black enters his men in the white board and moves around in the same manner.

Rules are the same as for backgammon, except that you

can move any man you want to at any time, whether or not you may have men to bring in.

In addition, the roll of 1–2—acey-deucy—is an especially valuable roll. You begin by playing your ace-deuce. Then you play any number four times (in other words, you pick any double you wish). Then you get an extra roll. And if this extra roll is also 1–2 you get the same extras with it.

Early game strategy in acey-deucy is to try to establish advanced points as quickly as you can, and if possible also establish adjacent points as base for a prime. If both sides develop primes right smack up against one another, the advantage lies with the prime that is farther advanced. Even if the man with the farther-advanced prime has to break his first, he will probably win the game; if he can hold his prime longer, he almost surely will win.

There is one bit of unusual strategy in acey-deucy that we consider rather sharp practice. A player who is getting the worst of the game will bring only fourteen men into play, holding the fifteenth (known as "Clammy") in his hand. Eventually his opponent will have to expose a man while bearing off. "Clammy" will hit one of these blots and the whole complexion of the game will change. It is sharp practice, but Navy men are supposed to be able to count to fifteen.

## Plakoto

A number of varieties of backgammon are popular in Greece. Regular backgammon is called *portas*, or "doors"; each point is one *porta* (and a prime of six points would be "all doors closed," we have a hunch).

Another version of the game played in Greece is usually called *plakoto*. The inner and outer boards are the same as in regular backgammon, but all fifteen of white's men are on the black one point, and all of black's men are on the white one point opposite (i.e., both to the *right*, if you are sitting in white's chair, and to the left if you're sitting in black's, opposite). All the men must again move the full twenty-four points, in the same direction as they do in regular backgammon.

In plakoto you can stop on an opponent's man, but you

can't take him off the board. However, as long as you leave your man on him, he cannot move.

The advantage you gain by pinning a man is far greater than you gain by hitting a blot in backgammon. When you hit a blot, that man can be brought into play again. When you pin a man he is out of play until you remove the pin. Furthermore, you have full control of the point in question and can move additional men to it. As an example of the value of an early pin, suppose that you roll 4–3 as the opening play of the game. Your correct play is to move two men forward to the black four and five points, since you want to start making as many points as possible quickly. Black proceeds to roll double 5. He uses all four 5s to move one man to pin your blot on his four point. If the game were played using the doubling cube, he would have a doubling advantage irrespective of your next roll; as it is, he is at least a two-to-one favorite to win the game and a gammon is quite likely.

Except for the initial setup and the pinning of blots, all rules are the same as in backgammon. Your strategy is to establish as many points as possible as quickly as you can, unless you get a chance to pin a man or men.

## Gioul

This game probably originated in Turkey, but it is played throughout the Middle East. The men are set up and move as in plakoto, but there are no blots and one man stopping anywhere controls the point he is on, as in moultezim.

The distinctive feature of this game is the rolling of doubles. When a player rolls a doublet, he plays that number four times; then he plays the next higher doublet in the same fashion, and so on until he has played double 6. Thus a throw of double 1 entitles the lucky player to play four aces, then four 2s, then four 3s, then four 4s, then four 5s, and finally four 6s.

Obviously if you get a chance to play such consecutive doubles early in the game, it is most advantageous, but in the middle game when your opponent controls a lot of points (remember one man is enough for control) the chances are that you won't be able to complete your move.

If so, you forfeit what you can't play to your opponent. Thus, if you roll double 2 and after playing four 2s and a 3 find that you can't play a second 3, you lose the rest of your move; but instead of just losing it as in backgammon you lose it to your opponent who now proceeds to play the other 3s, the 4s, 5s, and 6s. If he can't complete the play, the rest of the moves are not made and he takes his next roll.

Planning strategy in this game consists mostly of preparing a position in which you will be able to move doubles (principally 5s and 6s) while blocking your opponent from doing the same. In this case it won't matter which one of you throws a double. You will get all the play if you roll it and most of the play if he does. With all this complicated planning the game is likely to be far slower than other forms of backgammon.

## Summary

We have included these other games in case you should ever get tired of regular backgammon and want to try a substitute. Our own experience is that there is so much variety to the regular game that we never tire of it.

# 18

# ETIQUETTE

Good etiquette makes for good backgammon and good fun. Poor etiquette leads to arguments, bad backgammon, and no fun at all.

Unlike other games where practically all arguments can be settled easily, there are many occasions in backgammon in which each player will be certain that he's right.

As an example, suppose that midgame you roll 5–4; you move a man, correctly, from the black eleven point to your five point, and then pick up your dice. You have done everything properly and correctly, but your opponent doesn't think so.

He may have misread your dice and thought that you rolled 5–3. Or he may have thought that your man came from his ten point, not his eleven point. In either of those instances your correct play would have been to bring that man to your six point, not to your five point. If you have several men on the point you moved to and also on the adjacent points, then it may be confusing to him just exactly where the man you moved should have gone.

In this case you followed the rules carefully, and you are certain that you did not make a mistake. Therefore you should insist that the man you moved must stay where he is, and your opponent should accede gracefully.

But suppose that you roll your dice, then reach for your man with one hand while scooping up the dice with the other, and then drop your man carelessly somewhere in your board. Your opponent should be excused for questioning what your dice showed, where your man came from, where you placed him, or all three, and if he insists that you were wrong, you should give in to him.

You actually had broken no rule, but you had violated proper etiquette, since you had given your opponent no real chance to check the correctness of your play.

We urge you to make all plays very carefully, with full observance of such proprieties as *using just one hand to move the men* and *leaving your dice strictly alone until all moved men have been quitted.* "Smart-alecky" play, such as moving two men at the same time, one with each hand, deserves any penalty that it may cause you. The fact that your play is accurate doesn't make you right. If your opponent raises some objection, you are obliged to accede to him, and you have only yourself to blame.

The rules provide that your play ends when you start to pick up your dice, so that if you do this before completing your move, your opponent can either compel or forbid the completion of the move.

You should enforce this rule, with one exception. That exception occurs when your opponent rolls something like 4–1, moves the 4, picks up that die and leaves the die showing the ace untouched while he studies how to play it. We deplore this kind of confusing play—even though it falls within the rules because your play is not technically finished until both your dice are back in the cup.

The rules also provide that if a player rolls before his opponent has completed his play by starting to pick up his dice, the opponent may accept the roll or compel the offender to roll over again.

This rule should not be abused, however. Let's say white starts with 3–1. He is going to make his five point, and everyone knows it; if black rolls too soon, his roll should stand. Or let's say white is bearing off and rolls 6–5. His six point is empty so he *must* bear two men from his five point. If black rolls too early, his roll should stand. One should abide by the rules, but no one should use the rules to gain an unfair advantage.

In some complicated positions you may actually move your men with the intention of studying the position this tentative move leaves, in order to decide between that play and some other. In such cases your opponent should not roll until you start to pick up your dice; but good etiquette also demands that when you make any tentative move you announce that you are thinking it over.

There is a further reason why you should make such an announcement. Many times, even in the most expert games, we have seen a player move tentatively and then replace the men he has moved incorrectly—or else his opponent thinks that they have been put back wrong. If you announce in advance that you are only moving tentatively, your opponent will concentrate on the original position and there will be far less risk of argument.

When you move any man, you should always be careful to place him squarely on the point he goes to, in order to avoid later argument as to where he is. Also, in making your moves, make sure that your opponent is able to check that you are moving correctly. When you roll a double, if you want to move two men at once, be careful to make sure that your opponent knows where they started from; and always be sure to make each of your four plays in such manner that your opponent will be certain that you've made exactly four moves and not three, five, or six.

There is even an etiquette to rolling your dice. You should shake them well and, while it is all right to hold your hand over the mouth of the dice cup while shaking, make sure to remove it before the actual roll.

As we remarked before, in a chouette it is your privilege to consult with the captain, but don't be obstreperous about it and don't feel called upon to advise on each and every roll. Let the captain make most of the decisions. And as captain, don't feel obligated to ask advice on each and every roll, but when there may be a problem take time out and ask your partners. Remember, it will make the game unnecessarily and unpleasantly slow if everyone goes into a huddle over each play.

The captain, of course, has full right to make all decisions except that he can't accept a double for his partners. On the other hand, the captain should *not* insist on doubling the game when a majority of his partners don't want to do so (see Modification 3 in the last chapter).

Backgammon can be a most annoying game. Your opponent can roll a couple of key doubles and transform a sure loss into a win, or you can get a man on the bar and fail to come in for several rolls as your opponent improves his position with each free play he gets. We don't know of anyone who doesn't show his annoyance at times, but you should try not to show it too vigorously. It doesn't do the least bit of good to bang down your dice cup or throw the dice out the window. You are entitled to get a trifle mad, but do so reasonably and pleasantly.

The best you can do about your own bad dice is to shake them hard and extra long. It doesn't really do any good, but it isn't bad manners and it does give you a chance to blow off steam and cool down. As for your opponent's good dice, the rules (Law 6b) provide that you can change dice at the start of any game and tell you how to go about it. In some games you are allowed to change dice in the same manner at any time. We don't like this, since such changes in the middle of the game slow up the play and achieve no real good. It is very unlikely that you will ever play with loaded dice, or with a man who can roll dice out of a cup and control them. In fact, it is very unlikely that you will ever play with a man who can roll dice out of his *hand* and control them, so just bear in mind that just as footballs take funny bounces, dice can take funny rolls—and that bad luck doesn't last forever.

As a final point, if you must put a drink on the table (hard or soft is all the same) be careful not to confuse it with the dice cup. Dice don't quench your thirst in the slightest, and if you roll the drink it's even more frustrating!

# 19

# BACKGAMMON STORIES

Bad luck is likely to cause the hapless victim to lose his head, but our first story will be about the man who lost his head because of *good* luck.

The place was Persia. The time about 500 B.C. The King of Persia and one of his nobles were playing an ancient version of backgammon on a board rather similar to our modern board. The king had a good position, with all his men strategically placed. The Persian game was played with three dice, and the king now proceeded to roll 6–3–2. Upon studying the position, he found that he had to break three points and leave six blots. Instead of a probable win, the king was suddenly faced with a sure loss.

Then the noble made a serious mistake. He laughed— and lost his head. There is no report as to whether the king finished out the game against his heirs.

The late Sherman Stearns, one of the great bridge players of the 1930s, was also a pretty fair backgammon player, but he claimed to be cursed with extremely bad luck. He had lots of hard-luck stories, but the classic one was about the time he had been doubled to 32 in a running game, at a time when the doubler was actually a trifle behind. Sherman might have redoubled immediately, but he knew that his opponent was going to take almost any double, and anyway Stearns did not relish the possible loss of a 64 game. He bided his time until he found himself with one man on the five point and one man on the one point, while his opponent was left with four men. One of those four men was on the five point, so even if Sherman failed to get both men off with this roll, the other player could win only by then rolling double 5 or 6.

Sherman doubled to 64, his opponent accepted, saying, "You just rolled a double. I'm about due." He ignored the fact that Sherman could win the game with any twenty-three out of thirty-six possible rolls; and even if Sherman missed, he himself would need a roll of double 5 or 6.

So Sherman rolled and, sure enough, missed, whereupon the other player rolled his double 5 and won.

We consoled Sherman by telling him that he was lucky his opponent didn't redouble to 128!

Everyone has similar hard-luck stories. We have seen players roll the only number that will cost them the game time after time. We have seen a player with a sure gammon or backgammon coming up throw dice that force him to leave his last man as a blot. The blot is hit and his gammon has disappeared. The opponent fills his board and actually succeeds in winning the game, with fifteen men against one.

The most extraordinary case we know of occurred in Nassau not long ago. White had doubled against black's back game, and the back game had collapsed. Eventually white got down to two men on his two point. Black still had four men on the white one point, and his eleven other men were scattered around the board.

White rolled 5–1 and had to leave his last man on that two point. Black failed to hit that blot and the only way white could miss winning a gammon was to roll double 1. Sure enough he did. Given another chance, black came through with an ace and hit the blot.

Black still wasn't out of gammon country. He had to get his men together and keep white from getting around the board, but a series of good rolls by black and bad ones by white allowed this to happen. Finally, black filled his board and started to bear off. White kept failing to get on, and eventually black redoubled, in a position where poor white had no choice but to accept. Luck stayed with black and he won!

In all gambling games there is a loser's syndrome which causes people to keep on when behind and to go further and further into the hole. The doubling feature in backgammon makes this syndrome far more dangerous. *Psychologically, it is much easier to say "Let's start the cube at 2 or 4" than it is to say "Let's double the stakes."* In addition, this syndrome causes the loser to double too soon and to accept doubles which he should refuse.

Almost anything can happen when a player gets caught up in a loser's syndrome. The following incident occurred at one of New York's leading clubs. A young member of modest means started to play for five dollars a point against a rather overbearing, wealthy older member. Luck favored the younger man, but his opponent doubled and redoubled desperately, so that after an hour or so the youngster was five hundred dollars ahead.

The loser insisted on starting all games at 2 and practically bludgeoned the young man into agreeing. The next step was to move the cube to 4, then to 8, and eventually up to 64. None of this did the loser any good. He just lost more, and the eventual tab came to around a hundred thousand dollars.

The rich man, who had blustered and forced the stakes up, even against the young man's steady protests, now said, "I don't see why I should pay you. If you had lost, you couldn't have paid me." Then he offered a five-thousand-dollar settlement. The opponent, who had quietly stood the man's insults and had behaved most properly throughout, now replied, "I know I couldn't have paid a hundred thousand, *but I could have paid everything I might have lost*. You kept doubling to get even, and now you must pay the full amount you lost."

We are pleased to report that when the rich man had time to cool off, he did pay in full. Not that we approve of such high-stake gambling, but we do believe in paying gambling debts.

Our final story is about a young man of good family but poor character who figured out a nice racket and went to London to try his scheme.

He was attractive and a good backgammon player. His technique was to get hold of an easy opponent, preferably a lady with money of her own or a rich husband. He would suggest a game of backgammon for very low stakes, just to while away a little time. He was far too nice to play for anything except a very low stake.

Translating pounds into dollars, the stake he suggested was worth around a nickel a point. No one could win or lose much at five cents a point . . . but there was one little

235

gimmick. He suggested that in such a game it would be much more fun if each player could start with a good first roll. Therefore, if the first player did not like his first roll, he could roll again and again until something satisfactory turned up. Then, to make things even more interesting, each such extra roll would move the cube one notch higher. And, he added considerately, it would obviously be unfair if the second player didn't get the same option.

For a while these options would be used with moderation, and games would start at somewhere from 16 to 64. Then he would see to it that they moved higher and higher. The chances are that the victim would have no idea what was happening to her until the game would end, and she would be informed that she had lost a very large sum. Of course, he would say, it was a shame that their little "fun" game had gotten out of hand, but if he had lost he would have paid, so now what was she going to do about it? Usually, his victim would pay up, but eventually he decided to try his luck in New York.

The shark's first victim turned out to be a killer whale. The lady was young, attractive, rich—but also happened to be a very good backgammon player. Furthermore, she wanted none of this nickel stuff or optional doubles. She suggested a high stake, and the shark, who simply could not imagine that the lady could play backgammon in his league, accepted—and proceeded to lose many thousands of dollars to her.

He turned out to be even more adept at not paying than he had been at collecting!

# GLOSSARY

Here are definitions of terms commonly used in playing backgammon. The numbers in parentheses following some entries indicate the chapters in which further discussion will be found.

**Around the corner.** A man moved from your opponent's outer board into your own outer board; most commonly, moving one of the men on your opponent's twelve point to a point in your own outer board.

**Automatic doubles.** A modification of the normal rules, stipulating that the stakes are automatically doubled at the beginning of a game if both players, in tossing for first play, roll the same number. (7)

**Back game.** A strategy employed by a player who is so far behind his opponent that he sees no chance to win in a running game. He tries to get even farther back by exposing blots around the board and in general delaying his own progress. The idea is to be able to hold two points in his opponent's inner board while deploying other men so that they will be effective blocks against any blot or blots that he can hit in the end game. (10)

**Backgammon.** When a player wins the game by bearing off all his men before his opponent has taken off any men and still has one or more of his men in the winner's inner table or on the bar; also called a "triple game" since the winner scores three times the stake.

**Back men.** Men in your opponent's inner table; you begin the game with two back men on your opponent's one point.

**Bar.** The middle strip in the board that separates the inner and outer tables, running in length from one player's side to the other's. In most boards it is a raised partition. Also called the "rail."

**Bar point.** Each player's seven point; the first point in his outer table, next to the bar.

**Bearing off.** Removing your men from the board, according to the rolls of the dice. You can start bearing off only after all of your men are in your inner table. Also called "taking off," or "throwing off." (1)

**Block.** Any point on which two or more of a player's men sit; his opponent can't touch down or land on such a point. Also called "making a point," "a point that's been made," etc.

**Blocking game.** A defensive game, in which you try to make points in your opponent's path to impede his movement.

**Blot.** A single man on a point. He can be hit by one of your opponent's men, thereby sending him off the board to the bar. He must then wait there until you roll a number on which he can enter a point in your opponent's inner board. Until your blot has re-entered, you cannot move any of your other men on the board. A blot is often called an "exposed man."

**Board.** (1) The entire backgammon table.
   (2) One of the four divisions within the table; each player has an inner or home board, and an outer board—also called the inner table and outer table. (See Diagram 1, Chapter 1)

**Box.** The "man in the box" in chouette. The player who at the start of play rolls the highest number; in all later games, the winner of the previous game. The box plays alone against all the other players, who form a team. (12)

**Break a prime.** A prime is six points in a row that you have made anywhere on the board (thereby totally blocking your opponent's men from moving past them); breaking a prime means removing a man or men from one of these points and leaving a blot or a vacancy.

**Builder.** Each extra man (i.e., more than two) on a point, or else a blot, in a good position to help make another point.

**Captain.** In chouette, the leader of those playing against "the box." The captain rolls the dice, makes the moves, and decides when to double for his team, though they may advise him. At the start of play, the player rolling the second highest number is captain; at the end of the game he becomes "the box" if he wins, or goes to the bottom of the line if he loses. (12)

**Chouette.** A form of backgammon for more than two players. One man, "in the box," plays against all the others, who constitute a team. One member of the team is captain. He makes the moves in consultation with his teammates. (12)

**Closed board.** A prime that a player has made on all six points in his inner table. It is thus "closed" to any of his opponent's men stuck on the bar waiting to re-enter.

**Cocked dice.** The dice are cocked unless both stop flat in one board (on one side of the bar). If the dice are cocked there must be a rethrow. (1)

**Combination shot.** An opponent's blot that is more than six points away from one of your men, and that therefore requires a roll combining numbers on both dice in order to be hit by that man.

**Come in** or **come on.** Bring a man that has been knocked off onto the bar back on your opponent's inner board. A player may not move any other men on the board while he has a man on the bar. Also called "entering," "entering from the bar," "re-entering." (1)

**Consolation flight.** In an elimination-type tournament, players eliminated in the first rounds may play in another tournament called a "consolation flight" or "sympathy flight." (14)

**Contact.** Positions on the board in which all of each player's men have not yet gotten past all of his opponent's men; it is therefore still possible for one or both players to leave a blot. (5)

**Counters.** See "Men."

**Count the position.** To figure the total number of points (your count) you would have to move in order to bear off all your men (assuming no waste motion), and then comparing it with the number your opponent would need (his count). (6)

**Cover a blot.** Move a second man to a point holding one of your blots. You thus make that point, preventing your blot from being hit.

**Cube.** See "Doubling cube."

**Cup** or **dice cup.** The cup used to shake and throw your dice.

**Dice, die.** Plural and singular for the cubes used in casting. These are conventional dice (i.e., each die has six faces, marked with 1, 2, 3, 4, 5, and 6 dots).

**Direct shot.** An opponent's blot that is six or less points away from one of your men, and that therefore you might be able to hit with the number rolled on only one die; as opposed to the "combination shot" required to hit a blot seven or more points away.

**Double.** To increase the game stake to twice its previous size. (7)

**Double game.** A gammon, in which you win double the stake.

**Doubles** or **doublets.** The same number thrown on both dice; you then move that number four times. (1)

**Doubling cube.** The oversized die marked on each face thus: 2, 4, 8, 16, 32, and 64; used to double and redouble the stakes and keep score. Sometimes called the "doubling block," or simply "the cube." (1, 7)

**Early game.** The first stages of play. (8)

**End game.** The last stages of play. (9)

**Enter,** or enter from the bar. See "Come in."

**Exposed** man. See "Blot."

**Gammon.** When a player wins a game by bearing off all his men before the loser has been able to bear off any. The winner scores twice the stake.

**Hit.** Landing on your opponent's blot, sending him off the board to the bar. Also called to "knock off."

**Home board.** Same as "inner table" and "inner board": that section of the board comprising your points one through six. (See Diagram 1, Chapter 1)

**Inner board** or **inner table.** Same as "Home board."

**In the box.** In chouette, "the man in the box" plays alone against all the others, who play as a team. Also called "the box." (12)

**Knock off.** See "Hit."

**Lead.** The difference between the point count of the two players.

**Lover's leap.** The usual play if the first roll of the game is 6–5: moving one of your back men on your opponent's one point up to your other men on his twelve point. (2)

**Making a point.** Accumulating two of your men on a point; once you have "made a point" your opponent cannot touch down or land there.

**Man in the box.** See "Box."

**Men.** The discs, counters, or checkers that you move around the board in accordance with the numbers you roll on the dice. Each player has fifteen men.

**Nothing game.** A poor relation of the back game in which you hold several good points in your opponent's inner board but have all your other men too far forward in your inner board on the one, two, and three points; thus if you hit a blot, he can still come in and get back around the board easily. (10)

**Off the board.** When a blot is hit he is sent "off the board" to the bar.

**Outer board,** or **outer table.** That part of the board comprising a player's bar (seven) through twelve points. (See Diagram 1, Chapter 1)

**Pip.** A point in the board, of which there is a total of twenty-four.

**Point.** (1) Each of the twenty-four narrow triangles on the board, twelve on each player's side.
(2) Any of the above on which you have two or more men: you have then "made that point," and your opponent cannot touch down or move there.

**Point on a blot.** To move two men to a point occupied by your opponent's blot: you hit his blot while making that point.

**Position.** Your standing in the game relative to your opponent's. (6)

**Prime.** Six successive points you have made, anywhere on the board; your opponent cannot move his men past a prime.

**Rail.** A less commonly used term for the bar.

**Redouble.** Doubling the game stake after a previous double. (7)

**Re-enter.** See "Come in."

**Running game.** The position in which all of each player's men have either passed or are nearly certain of passing all of his opponent's men, at which point the game simply becomes a race to bear off all of your men first. (5)

**Safe, or safety.** Moving a second man to a point holding a blot, thus making that point "safe."

**Semi-back game.** A player who is behind in the count and gains possession of his opponent's four or five point, thus hampering his opponent while still trying to run with his other men. (1)

**Setup.** The arrangement of the men on the board at the beginning of the game. (See Diagram 1, Chapter 1)

**Staying back.** Keeping several men in your opponent's inner board; part of the back game or semi-back game strategy. (1)

**Sympathy flight.** See "Consolation flight."

**Table.** Board. "Table" by itself is rarely used today; but "inner table" and "outer table" are used as frequently as "inner board" (or "home board") and "outer board."

**Taking off.** See "Bearing off."

**Throwing off.** See "Bearing off."

**Triple game.** A backgammon, in which you win triple the stake.

## ABOUT THE AUTHORS

OSWALD JACOBY and JOHN R. CRAWFORD are very good friends and through the years have been amiable rivals in a variety of games. At backgammon there are seven international championships: Jacoby has won three, Crawford one. Both still play. Crawford has also won the Regency Cup championship. At one time, Crawford held five national bridge titles, and Jacoby was second to him in four of them. Crawford has also been a member of three of the five American teams to win the world's championship. Jacoby has won the world's championship once and is at present non-playing captain of the world's championship team, which includes his son James, with whom he also writes a bridge column. He has won more national bridge championships than anyone else. At other games, Jacoby will admit that Crawford is probably the best gin-rummy player in the world. But Jacoby is probably superior at casino and piquet. When it comes to bridge and backgammon, neither will concede to the other, but no one will do well against them if they play as partners.

Both authors have written other game books. Some of these are: (for Crawford) *How to Be a Consistent Winner in the Ten Most Popular Card Games, Crawford's Contract Bridge, How to Win at Canasta, Playing Canasta* and *Samba;* and (for Jacoby) *How to Win at Canasta, Oswald Jacoby on Poker, Oswald Jacoby on Gin Rummy, How to Figure the Odds* and *Mathematics for Pleasure.* Jacoby's most recent previous book is *Jacoby Modern— A System for the Seventies,* written with his son.